Examining and Facilitating Reflection to Improve Professional Practice

Examining and Facilitating Reflection to Improve Professional Practice

Ann Shelby Harris, Benita Bruster,
Barbara Peterson, and Tammy Shutt

ROWMAN & LITTLEFIELD PUBLISHERS, INC.
Lanham • Boulder • New York • Toronto • Plymouth, UK

Published by Rowman & Littlefield Publishers, Inc.
A wholly owned subsidiary of The Rowman & Littlefield Publishing Group, Inc.
4501 Forbes Boulevard, Suite 200, Lanham, Maryland 20706
http://www.rowmanlittlefield.com

Estover Road, Plymouth PL6 7PY, United Kingdom

British Library Cataloguing in Publication Information Available

Library of Congress Cataloging-in-Publication Data

Examining and facilitating reflection to improve professional practice / Ann Shelby
Harris . . . [et al.].
 p. cm.
 Includes bibliographical references and index.
 ISBN 978-1-4422-0443-0 (cloth : alk. paper) — ISBN 978-1-4422-0444-7 (pbk. : alk.
paper) — ISBN 978-1-4422-0445-4 (electronic)
 1. Teachers—In-service training. 2. Reflective teaching. 3. Professional learning
communities. I. Harris, Ann Shelby, 1939–
 LB1731.E87 2010
 370.71—dc22   2010010106

∞ ™ The paper used in this publication meets the minimum requirements of American
National Standard for Information Sciences—Permanence of Paper for Printed Library
Materials, ANSI/NISO Z39.48-1992.

Printed in the United States of America

To my three children: Karen, Wesley, and Robert, and their families, for their gifts of love, inspiration, and humor that make my life continually uplifted and enjoyable.—**Ann Harris**

To my wonderful husband, Barry, and our two beautiful children, Belinda and Billy, and their families, who are my inspiration in everything I do. Also, to my students, past and present, who continually motivate me to grow professionally.—**Benita Bruster**

To my family and friends. Their support and encouragement provide me with faith in myself, hope for the future, and the comfort of love and acceptance. Most of all, to Bergen, Erin, Leif, and their families, you give me purpose. —**Barbara Peterson**

This work is dedicated to my husband, Ron. His support and love have served as a constant encouragement during this endeavor.—**Tammy Shutt**

Contents

Foreword

The power of reflection as a tool for teachers' professional growth and for resolving instructional dilemmas is recognized widely. Teacher educators, professional development leaders (i.e., across the literacy, science, medical, and business communities), researchers, and accrediting agencies all value the potential of reflection for transforming teachers' practices and problem-solving abilities. As a collective, educators and researchers hold dear the works of reflection theorists, including Donald Schön, who wrote *The Reflective Practitioner: How Professionals Think in Action* (1983), almost three decades ago. Thinking about one's practice and problematizing take-it-for-granted actions is how teachers grow as professional leaders and excellent educators.

Schön's writing and the writings of many others have spawned decades of academic works in which theorists and researchers attempted to explain the illusionary practice of *reflective thinking*. Yet the paths to applying theories about reflective thinking to both research and practice have been murky and ill defined. Too often teacher educators and professional development leaders are left to their own devices for designing learning environments that encourage and deepen teachers' reflective capabilities. *Examining and Facilitating Reflection to Improve Professional Practice* was written to address the large gap we face in the professional development literature—how to support professional development in ways that improve professional practice. Ann Harris, Benita Bruster, Barbara Peterson, and Tammy Shutt provide a comprehensive and well-researched approach to designing environments that engage reflective thinking.

Applying theory to practice in the area of reflection is no small undertaking. Recent reviews of teacher education research (Cochran-Smith & Zeichner, 2005) and reading teacher education research (Risko, Roller, Cummins, Bean, Block, Anders, & Flood, 2008) led researchers to conclude that engaging professionals in an analysis of personal understandings about teaching and learning is difficult to achieve. Both prospective and practicing teachers, for example, tend to analyze problems literally with little attention to complexity of dilemmas, and thus, responses to instructional dilemmas tend to be ineffectual.

Frequently teachers have not been taught how to identify and analyze instructional problems from different perspectives; yet problem-solving abilities are both the goal and the processes required for effective reflections on practice. Some changes to the approach to reflection instruction have appeared within the last decade. For example, we (Risko et al., 2008) observed a shift from hands-off instruction that had limited impact on developing teachers' reflective abilities to forms of guided instruction that deepened reflective thinking. These forms of guided instruction included explicit expectations, modeling, and provision of continuous and specific feedback. Translating this research to practice, however, remains a weak link to the research evidence. With two colleagues, I recently conducted an informal survey of twenty recent teacher education studies (2005–2008) examining reflection instructional approaches and found that only 30 percent provided clear descriptions of how reflection strategies and skills were taught (Risko, Vukelich, & Roskos, 2009). Well-defined instructional methods for inviting and teaching reflection in order to develop teachers' reflective skills should be a top priority for our professional texts. And fortunately, providing explicit information on designing instruction, including methods that engage peer collaboration and digital technologies, was the goal of Ann Harris, Benita Bruster, Barbara Peterson, and Tammy Shutt when they wrote this book. They address quite specifically a gap in our professional literature.

And their work addresses instructional components that are identified repeatedly in the research literature. For example, an examination of a largely descriptive research literature produced several instructional features that appear especially supportive of prospective teachers' reflection development and learning (Risko, Vukelich, & Roskos, 2009). The four colleagues address these features specifically in the text that follows. They include: (1) *A well-articulated definition of reflection that serves to theoretically ground and guide instruction*; (2) *Clear instructional goals that set the direction for teaching and learning action;* (3) *The use of stated criteria against which the instructor examines or judges prospective teachers' reflection performances in oral and/or written contexts;* (4) *Multiple, multilayered opportunities to learn reflection concepts, skills, and dispositions in challenging yet achievable ways*; and (5) *Compelling content found in coursework and clinical or field experiences.*

We are fortunate to benefit from the thoughtful writing of Ann Harris and her colleagues and for their insights that provide a direction and promise for designing learning environments that support reflective problem solving and transforming professional development.

Victoria J. Risko, Professor
Language, Literacy, and Culture, Vanderbilt University

REFERENCES

Cochran-Smith, M., & Zeichner, K. (Eds.). (2005). *Studying teacher education: The report of the AERA panel on research and teacher education.* Mahwah, NJ: Erlbaum.

Risko, V. J., Vukelich, C., & Roskos, K. (2009). Detailing reflection instruction: The efficacy of a guided instructional procedure on prospective teachers' pedagogical reasoning. *Action on Teacher Education Research, 31*(2), 47–60.

Risko, V. J., Roller, C., Cummins, C., Bean, R., Block, C. C., Anders, P., & Flood, J. (2008). A critical analysis of the research on reading teacher education. *Reading Research Quarterly, 43*(3), 252–288.

Schön, D. A. (1983). *The reflective practitioner: How professionals think in action.* New York: Basic Books.

Preface

Examining and Facilitating Reflection to Improve Professional Practice is unique in many ways and is written to develop and strengthen the reflective thinking abilities of individuals. The book is specifically designed and organized for use in introductory foundations of education courses and continuing through content-specific methods courses for both preservice and in-service classroom teachers. Ideally, this book can be partnered with any courses for undergraduate and graduate classes that require students to use self-reflection, critical thinking, and problem-solving. The book also meets the needs of experienced teachers who are seeking advanced degrees and need to better understand reflective thought and practice to serve as instructional leaders.

The focus of this book on decision making and professional development also benefits the spectrum of professionals in business, medicine, social work, and nursing. Practical suggestions enable various individuals to understand and identify developmental phases of reflection, supported by theory drawn from research. The text offers guidance to help teachers and other professionals develop an awareness of the fluidity and developmental nature of reflection. One of the purposes of the authors in creating this text is to cause individuals to think in diverse ways and grow in their reflective process, ultimately improving their professional practice.

The contents of this book are essential to educators because most universities and schools across the nation have identified a set of national academic standards for all students to achieve for graduation. A standard on reflection is included in each set of national standards, and most professions encourage reflective practice. Among these national associations with such requirements are the:

- Interstate New Teacher Assessment and Support Consortium (INTASC),
- National Council for Accreditation of Teacher Education (NCATE),
- National Board for Professional Teaching Standards (NBPTS),
- International Reading Association (IRA),
- National Council of Teachers of English (NCTE), and
- Numerous other professional associations.

Individuals do not automatically know how to reflect, and there are limited resources available for instruction. Too many times, individuals have mistaken ideas about reflection, i.e., reflection is simply a listing of the day's happenings or summaries of events. This text is an easily accessible resource, a discussion and activities guide, and a support for use in reflection. The information and effective reflective strategies found in the text can be easily incorporated into most instructional activities or programs.

The scope of this book is to provide information that will fuel well-planned discussions and experiences to reinforce viewing reflection as critical inquiry, resulting in changes of thinking, beliefs, and actions. Reflection is a developmental process, with individuals entering the process at differing levels of conceptual understanding. The features that support clarification and comprehension of concepts follow:

- An overview at the beginning and a summary at the end of each chapter
- Case studies and scenarios of classroom practices
- Opportunities for group interaction in the form of *Pause to Think* activities
- Critical-thinking questions and probes
- Examples of each developmental phase of reflection and examples of reflections with specific characteristics that match each phase
- Chapter study questions and suggested problem sets/activities
- Bibliographies listed at the end of each chapter
- An alphabetical subject index

Supplementary teaching and learning tools have been developed to accompany this text. Please contact Rowman & Littlefield at textbooks@rowman.com for more information:

- A PowerPoint presentation
- An instructor's test bank of questions for each chapter

The chapters are arranged in a sequence of reflective content and activities. The underlying theme of the book is to educate individuals to become more reflective practitioners.

In chapter 1, a broad overview of the nature and purposes of reflective practice is introduced. The early researchers with their pragmatic theories as related to practice are briefly discussed. This chapter acquaints the reader with the national standards requirements for ongoing reflective thinking. The current trend of professional learning communities is introduced as a successful interactive reflective process.

In chapter 2, actively thinking and exploring reflection using multiple venues to improve practice is promoted. This chapter is used to introduce and emphasize the developmental aspect of reflection, coupled with supportive activities. Interactive strategies and activities emphasis the importance of using multiple ways of thinking as venues for individuals to develop and mature in the reflective process.

Chapter 3 is highlighted with key aspects of critical incident analysis by identifying and evaluating teaching dilemmas with authentic classroom scenarios. Case studies containing critical incidents are used as ways to evaluate reflective decision making. The chapter concludes with an exploration of the role of critical reflection in professional practice.

Chapter 4 is presented to introduce the concept of emerging literacies of technology, including wikis and blogs and their use as tools to actively encourage reflection. These emerging literacies provide individuals with opportunities to develop social and professional networks as a reflective mode for the future.

In chapter 5, the importance of the specific use of language and how dialogue between professionals can support and influence reflective practice is outlined. The use of dialogue and cognitive coaching are both excellent venues for improving reflection. The social negotiation of meaning is enhanced by analyzing dialogue within the context of blogging and reflective-style journaling.

Chapter 6 includes the phases of reflection and provides professionals with opportunities to read, discuss, and interact using critical-thinking prompts and questions. Suggested instructional applications are presented to help individuals become more reflective and analytical in their daily practice.

Chapter 7 is a valuable tool for instructional leaders and other professional leaders who want to become more familiar with effective reflective strategies. Techniques to analyze and use reflection in the evaluation process are presented. Implications of reflective practice and the culture of inquiry for leadership are examined using electronic portfolios and retrospective journals.

No matter what grade level or discipline, professionals and students across the nation are being asked to reflect upon their thoughts, processes, and actions of their practice. The focus of the text addresses how much, how often, when, in what context, and more importantly, why reflection is essential. Asking individuals to reflect without answering these questions makes the process of reflection more difficult. The objective of this book is to encourage and improve reflective thinking and practice among professionals.

Chapter One

Perspectives and Implications for Reflective Practice

Refection is considered central to all learning experiences enabling us to act in a deliberate and intentional fashion . . . [to] convert action that is merely . . . blind and impulsive into intelligent action (Dewey, 1933, p. 212).

OVERVIEW

In this chapter, the concept of reflection is introduced. Historical perspectives are explored, and current methods that prove to be successful for fostering reflective thought are established. Reflection is defined as a process that includes looking back on a situation and making informed decisions, then looking forward and assessing the consequences of those decisions. In this chapter, reflection is viewed as a necessary tool to enrich practice as it has been found to encourage and foster analysis, critical thinking, and professional change.

Reflection is discussed historically from Dewey's beliefs in 1933 to the current understanding of reflection. The importance of reflection is aptly demonstrated in state and national standards that have a component requiring reflective thinking.

Professional learning communities are introduced as one successful way for improving professional practice. As peers interact with each other, they gain a broader perspective of the reflective process. As professionals observe events and situations from multiple viewpoints, they learn from each other different and alternative ways to improve their practice.

Perspectives on the Reflective Process

Listen to the voices of professional educators attending a national conference who were asked to express their thoughts about reflection. Their responses to the prompt "Reflection is . . ." included:

"... looking back in order to move forward,"
"... learning from our mistakes,"
"... hard,"
"... necessary to improve practice,"
"... sorting through my beliefs and principles,"
"... reviewing,"
"... thinking and recalling information, images, and so on."

The core beliefs about reflection among these experienced educators are evident through these responses. Often assumed is that the act of reflection itself is sufficient to promote a clear understanding of situations. Individual descriptions of reflection, however, vary greatly. Also, it is difficult to determine how these individuals reflect on a given situation. The responses suggest their understanding of reflection is merely glancing back at a lesson or situation. Descriptions of reflection used by the experienced educators cited above do not provide evidence of how these educators used reflection to improve their practice. Without more information, it is not evident if they used reflection to develop new perspectives or used reflection to analyze possible factors that resulted in the best course of action.

Pause to Think . . .

Working in a small group, do this exercise. Complete this phrase with at least two different words:

Reflection is . . .

Discuss the different responses in your group. How are your responses different, and why?

INTRODUCTION TO REFLECTION

Reflective Practice

Learning how to do something and doing it well involves thinking about what is being learned or experienced and developing a deeper understanding.

Dewey (1933), in the beginning quote of this chapter, referred to this process as reflection. He described reflection as central to all learning. In many professions, and especially in the teaching profession, reflective practice is considered key to professional growth and development.

Reflective practice facilitates the ability to learn from experience. Learning, especially in a professional context, requires an introduction to theory paired with opportunities to apply that theory to real situations in the field. Professional situations are often complex and may include dilemmas that might not be easy to resolve. Practitioners must draw on theoretical knowledge, previous experience, and knowledge of the current situation to determine the best course of action. Sometimes decisions must be made immediately, and individuals have little or no time to ponder alternatives but quickly come to a conclusion based on prior experiences. Other times, a decision can wait until later. Individuals then have time to consider possibilities before deciding the best course of action. In both instances, individuals are participating in reflective practice.

The basic premise behind reflective practice is that individuals' actions are guided by what they have learned from previous experiences. This idea is demonstrated as a teacher modifies and reteaches a lesson after reflecting. This example demonstrates a *thoughtful* examination of practice that leads to immediate change.

Reflective professionals have the ability to think about their behaviors and make judgments about them. In contrast, Valli (1997) suggested that professionals who are unreflective are limited in their ability to make change. They remain as skilled technicians who have not developed the intellectual and moral capacities to make wise decisions or consider the consequences of their actions. Unreflective individuals rely on routine behaviors and are guided more by impulse, tradition, and authority rather than by reflection (Valli, 1997).

Pause to Think . . .

Describe a time when you tried something that was not as successful as you planned.

After trying it again, list the changes you made.

What did you take into consideration when making the changes?

Unlike Valli's description of unreflective professionals, truly reflective practice is defined as the process of making informed and logical decisions, then assessing the consequences of those decisions. Reflection is a complex process of thinking and learning that involves at least two types: implicit reflection and explicit reflection.

Implicit Reflection

Implicit reflection refers to the way individuals think and resolve dilemmas. Dilemmas are often characterized as ill-structured problems having more than one solution. Jonassen (1997) referred to ill-structured problems as "problems in professional practice that possess multiple solutions and contain uncertainty about which concepts, rules and principles are necessary for the solution or which solution is best" (p. 65). Implicit reflection determines how a person interprets an event based on previous experience or personal belief.

Professionals are often faced with problems that are not easily solved. For example, in a classroom, a student accuses someone of stealing; however, the teacher did not observe the event. The teacher has the dilemma of determining the truth. No clear direction on how to resolve this situation is available, and the teacher must rely on prior experiences and knowledge about the situation and the students involved to arrive at a logical resolution.

Pause to Think . . .

List as many incidents as you can that describe situations (dilemmas) that are not easy to resolve.

In a group, discuss your list and talk about how you might reflect on each situation and what actions you will use to resolve the dilemmas.

Discuss your reasons (rationale) for why you made the decisions you made to solve the problem.

Explicit Reflection

The specific aspects of implicit reflection are also included in explicit reflection, namely using prior experiences and personal beliefs. Additionally, explicit reflection refers to the thinking that could be described as a form of metacognition in which individuals think about their actions, experiences, or beliefs (Zeichner & Liston, 1996).

Metacognition occurs, for example, when a teacher may be asked to reflect on a lesson that was taught. The teacher must recall the specific lesson and provide a rationale for changes that are needed for improvements. Using explicit reflection, the teacher visualizes the lesson and analyzes actions and beliefs about the lesson. Additionally, the teacher examines personal assumptions about the lesson that influenced decisions about how the lesson was taught. Explicit reflection involves a more critical analysis of a situation that enables an individual to act *in a deliberate and intentional manner*, as Dewey (1933) suggested.

HISTORY OF REFLECTION

Although many educators agree that reflection is an essential aspect of good professional practice, theorists have defined the concept of reflection in many different ways. John Dewey (1933) suggested assumptions and beliefs are examined through reflective thought to be sure they are grounded in logic, evidence, or both. Consequences related to particular reflections are implied. Dewey's notion of reflection defined reflection as a process of hunting, searching, or looking for material that leads to more thoughtful consideration.

Fifty years later, Schön (1983) recognized reflection as an important vehicle for the acquisition of professional knowledge. Schön introduced the concept of reflection-in-action, reflection-on-action, and reflection-for-action.

Reflection-in-Action

Reflection-in-action is spontaneous, and there is little or no time to step back and reflect. A decision must be made immediately. For example, a doctor caring for a patient in the emergency room in a life-and-death situation would require reflection-in-action. Immediate decisions must be made that draw on the expertise of the individual.

Reflection-in-action is difficult for most beginners (novices) in any profession because it requires prior experience and expertise in order to maintain the flow of the event. A novice seldom has the background or knowledge to resolve a dilemma without hesitation.

Reflection-on- and for-action

Reflection-on-action and for-action are closely aligned with Dewey's notions of reflection as looking back at an event. Reflection-on-action takes into consideration the context of the event by:

• analyzing the circumstances of the event, including personal biases or misunderstandings.

- planning actions based on careful consideration of all the information.
- guiding future actions.

Reflection-for-action is the desired outcome for the first two types of reflection. Reflection-for-action engages the professional in reflection to guide future actions.

STATE AND NATIONAL EDUCATIONAL DIRECTIVES FOR REFLECTION

Regardless of the type of reflection, the concept has become an expected component of professional development for teachers. Nearly all states have developed their own set of professional teaching standards, detailing what is expected for teacher licensure and professional growth. State and national standards have a required component for reflection. This component changes the way teachers think about their teaching, resulting in change. Additionally, reflective practice changes the way schools operate by providing opportunities for reflection and revision of curriculum. Education in public school districts and universities are required to implement state standards, and most of them have chosen to adopt one or more of the national standards. Among the national standards typically adopted by most universities are

- National Board for Professional Teaching Standards,
- Interstate New Teacher Assessment and Support Consortium,
- National Council for Accreditation of Teacher Education.

National Board for Professional Teaching Standards

National Board for Professional Teaching Standards (NBPTS) was established in 1987. Responding to national apprehension about teacher quality and concerns about strengthening the teaching profession, NBPTS developed standards for the advanced certification of highly skilled veteran teachers. The National Board established five core propositions as guidelines for what accomplished teachers should know and be able to do.

Proposition 4, and specifically subset 4.3, addresses the need for reflective practice.

NBPTS Proposition 4:

Teachers Think Systematically about Their Practice and Learn from Experience

Proposition 4.3 specifically states:

National Board Certified Teachers critically examine their practice on a regular basis to deepen knowledge, expand their repertoire of skills, and incorporate new findings into their practice (NBPTS, 2007, p. 2).

Interstate New Teacher Assessment and Support Consortium

In 1987, the Interstate New Teacher Assessment and Support Consortium (INTASC), a program of the Council of Chief State School Officers, crafted model standards for licensing new teachers. The INTASC standards provided a model policy that states can use as a resource to align their own teacher licensure requirements. Regardless of the subject matter or grade level, the INTASC standards address essential knowledge, skills, and dispositions necessary for effective teachers. Ten core principles of teaching knowledge presented by INTASC exist.

In Principal #9, the professional aspects of reflective teaching are acknowledged.

INTASC Principle #9

The teacher is a reflective practitioner who continually evaluates the effects of his/her choices and actions on others (students, parents, and other professionals in the learning community) and who actively seeks out opportunities to grow professionally (INTASC, 1992, p. 31).

National Council for Accreditation of Teacher Education

Complementing the NBPTS and the INTASC is the National Council for Accreditation of Teacher Education (NCATE). In 1954, NCATE was founded as an independent body responsible for accreditation in teacher education to establish high-quality teacher preparation programs. In 2000, NCATE designed *The Program Standards for Elementary Teacher Preparation* for enrollees in NCATE-accredited elementary teacher preparation programs.

Candidates' ability to reflect and evaluate professional growth is addressed in Standard 5b.

NCATE Standard 5b

Candidates are aware of and reflect on their practice in light of research on teaching and resources available for professional learning; they continually

evaluate the effects of their professional decisions and actions on students,
parents and other professionals in the learning community and actively
seek out opportunities to grow professionally (NCATE, 2000, p. 20).

The expectation of reflective practice as demonstrated by national teaching
standards has emerged as a common set of directives for teachers in school
districts and universities. The reflective component in each of these national
standards (NBSTS, INTASC, and NCATE) encourages teachers to record,
analyze, and make changes that are needed in the classroom.

Pause to Think . . .

Individually, go to your state Board of Education website on the Internet:

1) Find the teacher licensure standards for your state.

2) List the standard that deals with reflection.

Now, in a group, have each person find one additional state with a reflection standard.

1) Compare the different state requirements in regard to reflective
practice.

2) Discuss the differences with your group.

REFLECTION IN PROFESSIONAL LEARNING COMMUNITIES

Thus far, the discussion has focused on the definition, the history, and the
national and state directives for reflective practice. The importance of reflecting on individual situations in order to determine the best course of action
(reflection-in- and on-action) has been examined.

A concern among educators is the isolation experienced among new and
beginning teachers who teach in classrooms alone without the support of
other, more experienced teachers. Isolation from other teachers has been
cited as one cause for teachers leaving the profession. Using data collected
in 2003, the Schools and Staffing Survey (SASS) in education revealed
that 30 percent of new teachers left the profession by the end of their third
year (Ingersoll, 2003). For teachers in urban schools, the attrition rate for

new teachers was more than 50 percent by their third year (Henke, Zahn, & Carroll, 2001). Therefore, more than half the teachers in urban schools are new hires to the school, and they likely are inexperienced (Pirkle & Peterson, 2009).

Without guidance and an understanding of the reflective process, inexperienced professionals often suffer self-doubt when faced with challenging teaching situations. Without a supportive environment in which to reflect, new professionals burn out and leave the profession after only a few years. Improving reflective practice will engage professionals in developing new knowledge and awareness while promoting stronger self-efficacy in teaching.

Professionals who feel isolated in their practice need opportunities for dialogue with other professionals to help them remain engaged in ongoing reflection. Professionals, and especially teachers, need to keep pace with advances in technology and changing requirements in the workforce. Administrators in schools recognizing the need for dialogue among teachers are forming groups called Professional Learning Communities (PLCs), composed of individuals with common interests in improving teaching practice.

Professional Learning Communities are defined as connections between individuals' quest to build knowledge from personal experience through discussions among members of a community of learners (Scardamealia & Bereiter, 2006). The goal of the PLC is to intentionally advance knowledge by reflective discussions among peers. In this community, new learning is valued and constructed through experience and reflection. Isolation is removed in favor of collaboration and interaction among teachers. The environment of a Professional Learning Community is supportive and nurturing.

Pause to Think . . .

How can Professional Learning Communities support and improve professional practice?

In a small group, discuss the need for reflection in the workplace.

Reflection as a tool for learning has powerful implications, yet its full potential is realized only if the professional community supports a culture of learning. An environment most conducive to learning is open to new perspectives and is encouraging for the ongoing development of knowledge. Reflective thinking must be encouraged and supported to accomplish the ultimate goal of improved professional practice.

CHAPTER SUMMARY

Developing new insights through reflective practice is key to professional growth. Reflection is a thoughtful response to decisions made either during or after an incident. Recent emphasis on the need for reflection in professional decision making has been mainly inspired by the work of Dewey and Schön. Both theorists suggested the approach to facilitate the complex process of learning to bridge the gap between theory and practice.

In the context of their work, professionals make hundreds of decisions daily on instances that require them to reflect. These instances compel individuals to arrive at judgments and respond to particular problems or dilemmas. Individuals must:

- consider all the factors.
- develop possible solutions.
- weigh the consequences.
- determine resolutions.

Professional Learning Communities are one way individuals are making reflective decisions, through collaborating, discussing, and gaining insights into the complex nature of their work.

CHAPTER STUDY QUESTIONS

After reading this chapter, work in small groups to discuss these questions with your peers:

1. What is your definition of reflection?
2. Why is reflection useful in promoting professional decision making?
3. What factors should influence the way you reflect in different situations?
4. What do you take into consideration when you reflect?
5. What are Professional Learning Communities?

PROBLEM SETS/ACTIVITY

Working in a small group, read the following scenario and answer these questions.

1. What different actions might Mr. Garcia have taken?
2. Support your reasoning.

3. How will this situation inform Mr. Garcia's decisions and actions in the future?

Mr. Garcia is a first-year teacher using a token system as a form of classroom management. Actual money was used for the tokens. He noticed that Ling was passing a token to one of her friends, Becky. Mr. Garcia was aware that no student should be getting a token on this particular day. He needed to think on his feet. When he saw Ling pass a token to Becky, he became alarmed and needed to act quickly.

1. His first thought was, "rules are rules. . . . They broke the rules."
2. His next thought was, "The teacher needs to be in control."

At that point, Mr. Garcia confronted the girls, who denied any wrongdoing. He felt challenged in several ways at once. Mr. Garcia:

• needed to responded immediately when he observed a behavior that he considered morally wrong,
• believed the girls should have some consequence for their behavior,
• felt unsure of the school policy for this type of misconduct.

Mr. Garcia was conflicted because it was the end of the school day, and he was responsible for dismissing the class. He made a hasty decision to keep the girls after school but soon discovered that the girls rode the bus and had no way home. Next, he wrote a discipline referral to the principal that resulted in a Saturday detention and a call home to the parents. The parents disagreed with the consequences and believed them to be unfair. The parents accused Mr. Garcia of being insensitive and biased against their daughters.

BIBLIOGRAPHY

Dewey, J. (1933). *How we think: A restatement of the relation of reflective thinking to the educative process.* Boston: Heath.

Hatton, N., & Smith, D. (1995). Reflection in teacher education: Towards definition and implementation. *Teaching and Teacher Education, 11*(1), 33–49.

Henke, R., Zahn, L., & Carroll, D. (2001). *Attrition of new teachers among recent college graduates.* Washington, DC: National Center for Education Statistics.

Ingersoll, R. M. (2003). *Is there really a teacher shortage?* Center for the Study of Teaching and Policy, University of Washington, http://depts.washington.edu/ctpmail/PDFs/Shortage-RI-09-2003.pdf (Retrieved June 9, 2009.)

Ingersoll, R., & Kralik, J. (2004). The impact of mentoring on teacher retention: What the research says. Retrieved October 13, 2009 from http://www.ecs.org.

Interstate New Teacher Assessment and Support Consortium (INTASC). (1992). Model standards for beginning teacher licensing, assessment, and development: A resource for state dialogue. Washington, DC: Author.

Jonassen, D. (1997). Instructional design models for well-structured and ill-structured problem-solving learning outcomes. *Educational Technology: Research and Development, 45*(1), 65–95.

National Board of Professional Teaching Standards. (2007). Retrieved October 13, 2009 from http://www.nbpts.org.

National Council for Accreditation of Teacher Education. (2000). *Program standards for elementary teacher preparation.* National Council for Accreditation of Teacher Education: Author.

Peterson, B. R. (2007). The characterization of reflection by student teachers using the critical incident technique. *Dissertation Abstracts International, 69*(02), August 2008. (UMI No. 3301645).

Pirkle, S. F., & Peterson, B. R. (2009). Enhancing mentorship with podcasting: Training and retaining new and beginning teachers. *National Social Science Journal, 32*(2), 164. Retrieved October 13, 2009 from http://www.nssa.us.

Scardamalia, M., & Bereiter, C. (2006). Knowledge building: Theory, pedagogy, and technology. In K. Sawyer (Ed.), *Cambridge handbook of learning sciences* (pp. 97–118). New York: Cambridge University Press.

Schön, D. A. (1983). *The reflective practitioner.* New York: Basic Books.

Schön, D. A. (1987). *Educating the reflective practitioner: Toward a new design for teaching and learning in the professions.* San Francisco: Jossey-Bass.

Tripp, D. (1993). *Critical incidents in teaching: Developing professional judgment.* New York: Routledge.

Valli, L. (1993). Reflective teacher education programs: An analysis of case studies. In Calderhead & Gates (Eds.), *Conceptualizing reflection in teacher development.* Washington, DC: Falmer.

Valli, L. (1997). Listening to other voices: A description of teacher reflection in the United States. *Peabody Journal of Education, 72*(1), 67–88.

van Manen, M. (1977). Linking ways of knowing with ways of being practical. *Curriculum Inquiry, 6*(3), 205–228.

Yost, D., Sentner, S., & Forlenza-Bailey, A. (2000). An examination of the construct of critical reflection: Implications for teacher education programming in the 21st century. *Journal of Teacher Education, 51*(1), 39–49.

Zeichner, K., & Liston, D. (1996). *Reflective teaching: An introduction.* Mahwah, NJ: Lawrence Erlbaum Associates.

Chapter Two

Considerations for Reflective Thinking

We all acknowledge, in words at least, that ability to think is highly important; it is regarded as the distinguishing power that marks man from the lower animals. But since our ordinary notions of how and why thinking is important are vague, it is worthwhile to state explicitly the values possessed by reflective thought. In the first place, it emancipates us from merely impulsive and merely routine activity. Put in positive terms, thinking enables us to direct our activities with foresight and to plan according to ends-in-view, or to come into command of what is now distant and lacking. By putting the consequences of different ways and lines of action before the mind, it enables us to know what we are about when we act (Dewey, 1933, as cited in Archambault, 1974, p. 212).

OVERVIEW

The concept of thoughtful reflection is receiving unprecedented emphasis in today's classrooms. Again quoting the philosopher John Dewey (1933), the concept of *reflective thinking* is an "active, persistent, and careful consideration of any belief or supposed form of knowledge . . . ." (p. 9). Educators are now reviving an acknowledgment of the importance of *thoughtful* analysis of actions, activities, decisions, and strategies involved in reflective practice.

Classroom practice and reflective thought no longer can be deemed isolated and exclusive topics, but they must permeate all areas of teaching and learning. The goal of this chapter is to form a foundation for Dewey's "active, persistent, and careful consideration" embedded in learning how to reflect. Activities, scenarios, and instruction are used to focus on analyzing an event, an activity, or a dilemma from quite different perspectives. This

13

analysis creates opportunities for Dewey's beginning quote, which suggested "different ways and lines of action before the mind."

Information in this chapter promotes the examination and encouragement of reflective thought using various modalities. The presentation of these diverse venues is designed to encourage individuals to experience different thought patterns toward more effective reflection.

CONSIDERATIONS FOR REFLECTIVE THINKING

A bit of reflection is involved in almost everything everyone does. Done well, reflection is exciting and helpful at the same time; however, many individuals have difficulty expressing thoughtful reflection. Typically, individuals are expected to effectively reflect immediately following an assigned reading, an event, a situation, or their personal performance. Unfortunately, it is assumed that individuals *automatically* know how to reflect, develop deeper understandings, and adopt new perspectives. In most cases, this is not a realistic expectation because individuals typically have not developed adequate knowledge or skills for effective reflective thinking.

Reflection is customarily attempted by most individuals as a solitary activity, with limited or no instruction. Perhaps these limited reflective attempts are tried because little information is available explaining how reflection can be conceptualized and conveyed. A few individuals may complete a reflective activity with some degree of success, but most cannot. This scenario of unsuccessful reflection appears bleak indeed, but there are ways individuals can become more adept in the art and craft of reflective thought by regularly practicing, analyzing, and thinking in unique ways. Reflective thought must move beyond narrow preconceived ideas to recognize the truly symbiotic nature of individuals and situations.

In this chapter, reflection is recognized as not just a finished product but a rather tenuous process toward a completed product. Ross (1990) contends the reflective process is composed of the following:

- Recognizing educational dilemmas.
- Responding to a dilemma by recognizing both similarities in other situations and the unique patterns of the particular situation.
- Framing and reframing the dilemma.
- Experimenting with the dilemma to discover the implications of various solutions.
- Examining the intended and unintended consequences of an implemented solution and evaluating it by determining whether the consequences are desirable (p. 98).

The main focus of the reflective process begins in directing thought patterns to "transform a situation in which there is experienced obscurity, doubt, conflict, disturbance of some sort, into a situation that is clear, coherent, settled, harmonious" (Dewey, 1933, pp. 101–102). Initially, in this chapter the process of when, where, and how to reflect is discussed. Secondly, obstacles that hinder the process will be identified. Suggestions will be given that aid in minimizing or eliminating the obstacles. Lastly, developmental supports are described and designed to foster, influence, and promote the development of reflective thought. These supports rely on Ross's (1990) framing and reframing the dilemma, experimenting with the dilemma, and examining the subsequent consequences (p. 98).

TIMES TO REFLECT: WHEN, WHERE, AND HOW

When does and where should reflection take place? Further elaborating on Schön's (1983; 1987) theory, Schön stated that reflection takes place automatically as a part of everyday occurrences. He termed this process as *reflection-in-action* that occurs without persons' thinking about the fact that reflection is happening. The following is an example of an automatic reflection-in-action:

> As the teacher read aloud to her kindergarten students, she noticed the children were squirming in their seats during the story about baby chickens. She quickly asked the children to stand up and walk around the room imitating chickens, i.e., with arms bent to form wings, feet moving to imitate scratching in the dirt. After a few minutes of this *energy break*, the children were ready to sit down and listen again.

The teacher recognized the visual signs that the young children were tiring of sitting and needed a physical break. Of course, this type of reflection-in-action will vary in its effectiveness because of the prior knowledge and skills of individual teachers.

Pause to Think . . .

Read the following scenario and think back to a time when you were beginning a new position. Have you had an experience when you automatically used reflection-in-action to resolve a problem? Share your experience with others.

Example A. Eloise, a novice teacher, might use reflection-in-action by quickly thinking: "I know all this science content, but when an eighth-grade girl is not interested, rolls her eyes and asks 'Why do I have to know all this stuff?' I don't know what to say." The response that Eloise chose from her knowledge and skills was to ignore the girl's question and continue with her science lecture. *(The action in this scenario demonstrates ineffective reflection-in-action, showing a definite disparity between content knowledge and classroom situation control.)*

How does a teacher develop inner intuitiveness to know what actions should be or should not be a natural reflection-in-action for situations, such as Eloise's dilemma? Social tactfulness, i.e., knowing and doing what is best in a social circumstance, is compared by van Manen (1991) to *pedagogical tact* in a classroom. When discussing reflection-in-action involving successful, experienced teachers in the classroom, van Manen noted there are several creative or inventive abilities he termed *tact* involved in pedagogical practice:

1. A teacher who is tactful has the sensitive ability to interpret inner thoughts, understanding, feelings, and desires of children from indirect clues such as gestures, demeanor, expression, and body language. Pedagogical tact involves the ability to immediately see through motives or cause-and-effect relations. A good teacher is able to read, as it were, the inner life of the young person.
2. Pedagogical tact consists in the ability to interpret the psychological and social significance of the features of this inner life. Thus, the tactful teacher knows how to interpret, for example, the deeper significance of shyness, frustration, interest, difficulty, tenderness, humor, or discipline in concrete situations with particular children or groups of children.
3. A teacher with tact appears to have a fine sense of standards, limits, and balance that makes it possible to know almost automatically how far to enter into a situation and what distance to keep in individual circumstances. For example, it is a basic feature of educational intentionality that teachers always expect more and more from children. Yet, they must realize that they should not have expectations that, when challenged, children cannot manage to live up to. So, paradoxically, tact consists in the ability of knowing how much to expect in expecting too much.
4. Tact seems characterized by moral intuitiveness: A tactful teacher seems to have the ability of instantly sensing what is the appropriate, right, or good thing to do on the basis of perceptive pedagogical understanding of children's individual natures and circumstances (pp. 112–113).

As described by van Manen, reflection-in-action is an automatic response during an event or dilemma. Schön's reflection-on-action refers to retrospective thought after an event (1983; 1987). Retrospective thought includes the situation, persons involved, and supposed rationale for the occurrences. Killion and Todnem (1991) further clarified the process of reflection-on-action by adding the proactive aspect of reflection-for-action to include considerations and plans to guide future desired outcomes. By adding this element of the reflective process, reflective thought can now encompass "all time designations, past, present, and future simultaneously" (Killion & Todnem, 1991, p. 15).

Pause to Think . . .

Read the following scenario and think back to a time when you just wanted a *one-size-fits-all* or *pat answer* about something. At what point in your career, and how, did you realize that *pat answers* were not always possible in situations? After rereading van Manen's description of *pedagogical tact*, compose for the novice teacher, Eloise, an appropriate response to the eighth-grade girl. What particular perspective(s) of van Manen's helped you the most to develop your response?

Example B. Eloise asked her supervisor to "just tell me what to say to this eighth-grade girl who dislikes science." Eloise wanted a pat answer quickly—*one size fits all!* (Unless Eloise receives some instruction in reflection-on-action and reflection-for-action, her response to the eighth-grade girl's question may not vary from her previous one of ignoring the problem, resulting in frustration for Eloise and the girl.)

By implementing reflection-on-action and reflection-for-action (with adequate instruction), reflection-in-action improves and becomes *second nature*, knowing how to react with a desired outcome in mind. The old adage practice makes perfect becomes null. Without effective instruction, reflective thought only results in practice just makes more practice—no improvement, just a mechanical endeavor.

Dewey attempted to answer "How do we reflect?" by crafting several steps that an individual typically moves through in reflection, including:

- perplexity, confusion, doubt due to the nature of the situation in which one finds oneself;
- conjectural anticipation and tentative interpretation of given elements or meanings of the situation and their possible consequences;

- examination, inspection, exploration, analysis of all attainable considerations which may define and clarify a problem with which one is confronted;
- elaboration of the tentative hypothesis suggestions;
- deciding on a plan of action or doing something about a desired result (1933, pp. 494–506).

Individuals do not achieve the highest level of reflection immediately. Through proper instruction, modeling, experimentation, and constructive practice, however, a novice typically begins the journey toward insightful reflective thought.

OBSTACLES TO EFFECTIVE REFLECTION

Awareness of the obstacles to effective reflection aids in eliminating or nullifying those hindrances that radically deter the journey. Four obstacles are identified:

- Personal lack of patience,
- Time management problems,
- Fear of risk taking, and
- Improper structure of the reflective activity.

Personal Lack of Patience

The lack of patience with oneself in achieving and practicing reflective thought is an obstacle when understanding the recursive nature of reflection. Patience is the crucial quality of persistence and involves self-control and emotional restraint. The learning curve for reflection is not a continuous arching curve, but more representative over time of a recursive line with flat periods of stagnation or even regression. Most researchers agree that learning to reflect does not follow perpetual upward climbing curves or specific steps toward more insightful reflection, but developed over time, it is affected by personal traits as well as external environmental factors (Baird, Fensham, Gunstone, & White, 1991; Ross, 1989).

Reflection is a developmental process; therefore, instruction, guidance, and practice must occur all along the reflective learning curve. However, many individuals are extremely impatient, expecting their improvement to occur immediately and effortlessly. When working with preservice teachers on their reflective process, a disparity among individuals was noticed by their methods teachers. Shown in figure 2.1 are three hypothetical but typical

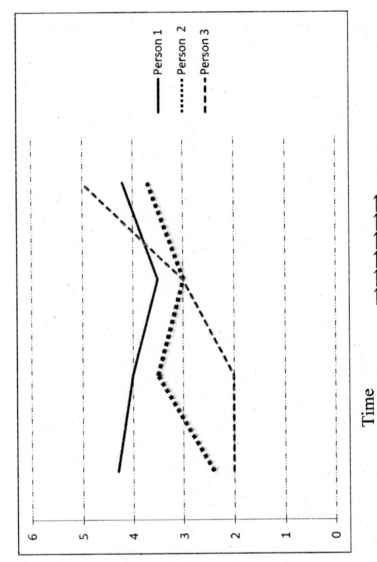

Figure 2.1. Learning Curve of Reflective Learning: Hypothetical Example

individuals, starting at differing ability levels of reflection and improving in the reflective process at different rates over time, with periods of stagnation and regression.

Time Management Problems

Closely aligned with patience is the factor of time management. For an individual to think analytically, planning and using time appropriately may be the most difficult obstacle to overcome. Immediate reflective thought-on-action that is closely aligned with the event, dilemma, or situation is especially difficult. The closer in time the reflective process is to the event, dilemma, or activity, the more helpful the reflective thought. This immediacy is sometimes not possible, however, because of other duties that interfere with the timely process. Some individuals have minimized this obstacle by

• jotting notes and reviewing them later,
• trying to recall the day's events hours later in a more relaxed atmosphere, and
• studying a list of individuals involved in the incident when there is more time to concentrate.

Fear of Risk Taking

Fear of risk taking ranks highly among the obstacles, especially written or oral reflection that requires sharing private thoughts of an individual with others and involves their feedback, which is considered critical. To help eliminate this obstacle, trust formed in a supportive relationship is necessary for successful reflection among the group or individuals involved.

Improper Structure of the Reflective Activity

The fourth obstacle can be an inappropriate structure or format of the assigned reflective activity. Most reflective situations involve structured writings, leaving little creativity and critical thinking among the individuals involved. Quite often, the written activity results in limited improvement in reflective thought because the instructor-generated questions or prompts influenced the degree and extent of thought. A few examples of a typical structured format might include these questions:

• What is the problem you believe needs improvement or change?
• What do you think caused this problem?

- Does this problem seem to be a constant one?
- How have you tried to solve the problem?
- Were you successful and, if not, why not?

Note how the questions are very restrictive rather than open-ended, leaving little room for critical analysis or thought. These questions also emphasize negative reflective thought, rather than giving equal emphasis to positive reflection. The writers sometimes feel restricted in their creativity and critical thinking and experience a loss of ownership when responding to prompts or questions (Greiman & Covington, 2007). The reflective writers are giving the perceived and instructor-expected response, robotically answering a set of someone else's questions rather than describing, critiquing, or analyzing their personal situation.

Pause to Think . . .

Using the four potential obstacles previously discussed, rank the obstacles that hinder your reflective process from the greatest to the least. Share with the group your ranking, supported by your rationale. Also list any different obstacles that you have experienced while reflecting.

DIFFERENT MODALITIES IN REFLECTION

Researchers have identified different modalities that are used in reflective thought and categorized them as

- written reflection,
- verbal reflection, and
- mental self-reflection (Bakhtin, 1981; Cowan & Westwood, 2006; Pedro, 2005; Risko, Roskos, & Vukelich, 2002; Webb, 1999).

The challenge for individuals is finding the right venue to cultivate the groundwork for individual reflective thought. Some individuals consider it surprising that there are several possibilities of venues for reflective thinking. Each method has its advantages and limitations, but all will achieve the primary goal of Ross's (1990) *framing and reframing* aspects of reflective thought. It is important to remember that individuals process information differently and have different strengths and abilities. The instruction supports and nurtures foundational reflective thought through varied experiences.

ALTERNATIVE SUPPORTS FOR REFLECTIVE THINKING

Reflective activities that provide strong supports must possess the following characteristics; they must be

- interesting. Individuals vary in their personal choices and ways of learning. Activities should appeal to a wide range of learner interests and learning styles.
- engaging. Individuals are motivated by hands-on activities that stimulate and provoke creative thought.
- challenging. Activities move learners to think beyond superficial observations to higher-order, reflective thought.

Supplying supportive venues (using different methods, materials to reframe the situation, event, or dilemma) aids in moving individuals toward more effective reflective thought. Writing using a matrix is presented as an excellent visual venue for reflective support. Four other different types of supports are identified for discussion:

- Double-Entry Journals
- Reflective Dialogue Journals
- Visual Metaphors
- Reflective Graphic Organizers

WRITING USING MATRICES

A reflective matrix is defined as a way to organize and display reflective thoughts using columns and rows. Matrices are typically used for representing connections between two or more ideas or concepts. The dimensions of the matrix refer to the columns and rows as shown in the following examples of double-entry journals and reflective dialogue journals.

Journal writing with some sort of matrix has long been accepted as a successful medium to develop reflective thought among individuals. The format of this writing can be diarylike, descriptive journals or logs, multientry journals, or portfolios. Most journal writing arises from assigned and very structured prompts in the matrix, which are planned to elicit thinking at various cognitive levels. Journal writing is typically a stand-alone activity; however, its primary objective lends itself to little or no feedback.

Much of the data to support reflective journal writing are anecdotal; however, when using journal writing as a beginning reflective tool, the noted benefits are:

- development of observational skills,
- reduction of stress and tension, and
- increased self-esteem (Callister, 1993; Dyment & O'Connell, 2003; Heinrich, 1992; Hill, 2005).

DOUBLE-ENTRY JOURNALS

Many ways exist to use matrices in reflective writing. An example of a multi-entry journal is the reflective double-entry journal, which includes the following directions:

1. Draw a line down the middle of a sheet of paper, forming two columns.
2. At the top of one column, write *Observations*. (These are just facts—what was seen and/or heard.)
3. At the top of the other column, write *Reactions and Interpretations*. (These are statements that involve personal experience, knowledge, and skills.)

An example of a reflective entry in a double-entry journal is shown in table 2.1. Diana, a fourth-grade teacher in her first year of teaching, identified a problem in her classroom. A suitable first step in reflection is recognizing a problem, dilemma, or event occurrence. Her reactions or interpretations were cursory—very little critical thinking demonstrated. Diana, however, has made a movement in the process toward reflective thought.

Table 2.1.   Double-Entry Journal Reflective Example (Fourth-grade Teacher)

Observations	Reactions/Interpretations
Several students are not turning in their workbooks to be graded.	I am concerned the students will cheat if I don't take up the workbooks and grade them. I need to find a way to motivate my students to turn the workbooks in on time.

Table 2.2. Reflective Dialogue Journal Example (Sixth-Grade Teacher)

WHAT?	SO WHAT?	NOW WHAT?
I did not have my lab supplies put together and ready to go for my science lesson. The lab supplies were all on one table and not divided out by groups.	There was chaos in the room with students trying to get all their supplies together for their groups. Not only were there a lot of students moving around but also they were talking and laughing as they assembled their supplies.	This is an example of poor planning and time management on my part. In the future I will have all the lab supplies on individual cookie trays in zipper-locked, plastic bags and labeled for each group. One member from each group will get a tray with supplies from the table and carry it back to the lab table.

REFLECTIVE DIALOGUE JOURNALS

A variation of the multientry journal that intentionally separates reflective thought even further is the reflective dialogue journal (see table 2.2). The directions are similar, except this time the paper is divided into three columns.

- The first column is labeled WHAT?. This column contains observations.
- The second column is labeled SO WHAT?. This column contains interpretations.
- The third column is labeled NOW WHAT?. This contains evaluation and corrective planning.

Note the contrast between the two journal entries. Tenesha is a sixth-grade teacher, also in her first year of teaching. Tenesha chose to also include the third column of this journal entry (NOW WHAT?), which requires evaluation and corrective planning; Tenesha moved toward more insightful, reflective thought by using this additional requirement of the reflective dialogue journal format. Tenesha evaluated one possible cause of her problem and added a plan for a better future outcome.

Pause to Think . . .

Share your experiences with different types of journal writing. Which type of journal writing appeals to you for reflection, and why?

VISUAL METAPHORS

Because individuals vary in the way they process information and differ in interest, strengths, skills, and abilities, this specific format of using visual metaphors for guiding reflective thought is multidimensional. Visual metaphors use all three modalities (written, oral, and inner thoughts) to enhance reflection and equally distribute the focus of the three modalities. It involves the power of analogy—comparing something that is quite familiar to something unfamiliar, thereby making the unfamiliar understandable. The use of metaphor occurs naturally in everyday life. Mezirow et al. (1990) illustrated this concept when he categorized metaphoric content into three domains:

1. Personal domain, such as characterizing a busy career as *being in a rat race*
2. Culture domain, for example, *going green* as being interested in preventing environmental pollution
3. Organizational domain, as *grass roots* being the lower levels of the political structure

Visual metaphors achieve more than just self-realization; they also achieve an awareness of an ongoing connection with an experience. This medium creates an aesthetic expression to elicit reflective thought, as depicted in the creation of a collage of metaphoric images. Collage creation is a combination of using literacy in the form of stories and dialogue combined with visual arts as a means to understand the surroundings of the situation and the individual's personal reaction to them. Collage combines thought patterns as represented by visual images rather than relying on written text or the spoken word. For some individuals, this medium may be the most appropriate and helpful means of expression.

Visual metaphors are considered a different spin on a complex idea. Information about self is revealed by individual choice of metaphors and the explanation for those choices. Metaphors can be particularly revealing of an individual's understanding of circumstances and values. The psychological impacts of metaphors are powerful to shape individuals' reflective thoughts and consequentially their actions.

To begin the process of developing visual metaphors, a group could be asked to form a collage to show their collective thoughts in answer to this question: "What words, phrases, or images come to mind when you think about reflective practice?" The open-endedness of the question elicits varying levels of thinking and personalizing the understanding of the question.

By working in groups, individual members better understand the expectations and opportunities of collage. Visual metaphors using collage are very adept in lending themselves to multiple possibilities and interpretations of meaning and knowledge. They involve putting knowledge and self-identity into images.

Pause to Think . . .

Try this activity individually: List the words, phrases, or images that come to mind when you think *about reflective practice.*

Visual metaphors are activities that focus all students on essential understandings of reflection, but at different levels of complexity, abstractness, and open-endedness. By keeping the focus of the activity the same, but accessing ideas at different levels of thinking, it is likely that each individual develops personalized ideas or understandings and is appropriately interested, engaged, and challenged.

Edgar (2004) suggested that the processing of putting thoughts into images generally has at least four stages:

- A descriptive stage where respondents "tell their story"
- Secondly, an analysis of the personal meaning of their experience and the symbols used
- Thirdly, an analysis of the thinking used to inform their imagery
- Finally, a comparative stage where the respondents share and compare their imagework with the rest of the group (p. 128).

In the following paragraphs, each of the four steps for constructing a metaphoric collage is enumerated. Descriptions for constructing a collage are based on the four steps for imagework by Edgar (2004). These descriptions and explanations illustrate and clarify more fully how to create a reflective collage after an individual has identified a dilemma, problem, or event for reflective thought:

- Step One. Tell the story. Search through magazines, newspapers, and so forth for images that depict how the individuals most strongly felt about an event or a certain aspect of an event. The size of the collage can be varied or simply 8 x 10 card stock. Collecting more than one image for a particular feeling, emotion, or aspect of an event is ideal. Online collages also can be made, using free electronic clip art that is not copyrighted.

- Step Two. Arrange images onto the paper or card. Overlapping shapes and some layering is permissible. Paste, glue, or attach the images to the paper or card. Check to make sure all images are secure. (Arrange images onto the document page, if using online sources.) Choose a title for each of the selected symbols. Check to see if any strong aspects of the reflective experience are overlooked. If so, go back and include them.
- Step Three. Compose a narration that summarizes the rationale for each of the symbolic images, using bold type for each image. The narration of the visual imagery makes this medium a strong producer of reflective thought. McIntosh and Webb (2006) stated that "it would appear that it is the decoding of 'the image' which has the greatest impact on learning—the thinking upon reflection itself, and the personal outcome gained through the process" (p. 13).
- Step Four. Share the reflective collages with the group, using the completed narrative as a script and showing the reflective collage. Meaning of the reflective dilemma, problem, or event is validated through discussion of the particular collage.

In the collage example in figure 2.2, a novice teacher reflects on her first year of teaching, particularly emphasizing her feelings and emotions. Notice how the chosen images and the decoding of each image dramatically convey the added dimension of personal emotions and feelings. This format does not stress all the other aspects of reflection previously addressed but more notably requires the individual to delve into feelings and emotions.

Pause to Think . . .

Name several ways you think using a collage as a visual metaphor offers professionals the groundwork for reflective thought.

REFLECTIVE GRAPHIC ORGANIZERS

Most individuals are familiar with categorizing a story into its basic literacy elements of title, characters, setting, plot, crisis/climax, and ending. Graphic organizers are historically used to display relationships between these literacy concepts. A reflective graphic organizer can be constructed using a few modifications of the literacy elements to Characters, Setting, Plot, Crisis/Climax, Outcome, and Desired Outcome (expanding upon the typical ending). By using similar literacy elements, a reflective graphic organizer format emphasizes the strong influence and impact of the

A Tree Blowing in the Wind. I sometimes feel so easily swayed by what reaction I should have to some negative conduct. Should I ignore some things or correct everything? Sometimes I do one thing and sometimes another.

A Little House Alone. I think the windows look scared, as I do sometimes when I am unsure. But all the lovely flowers (my students) make it all worthwhile.

Lightning Across the Sky. We will get our state test scores next week. Because this is my first year of teaching, I am hoping my scores will not be scary, like lightning is in a storm.

Prison Bars. Sometimes I feel I am closed in because of the required standards. There are so many ideas I would like to try, but there is not enough time to get everything required done and new activities I want to implement also.

Figure 2.2.   Example of a Reflection Collage (First-Year Elementary Teacher)

symbiotic nature of individual characters and the environmental setting on the outcome in a situation.

Begin the graphic organizer by composing a *Title* for the situation, event, or dilemma. The *Characters* are the persons involved. The *Setting* is the environmental situation. The *Plot* contains the targeted action for focus within the setting. The *Crisis/Climax* involves the most significant action or event within the plot. The *Outcome* is what actually happened to try to resolve the crisis or dilemma. The *Desired Outcome* would be an evaluation and typically a proposed solution with a more positive resolution.

As shown in table 2.3, the organizer is a flowchart format for easier text display. Flowcharts require individuals to consider each element related to the reflective process before moving to the next element. This type of graphic organizer helps individuals understand the process and how the reflective

Table 2.3. Example of a Reflective Graphic Organizer

Title of Event:	Homework Problems and a Note to a Parent

↓

Setting:	A Fifth-grade Classroom and Home

↓

Characters:	Kevin, a fifth-grade student, Kevin's mom, Dorothy Foster, and me (Mr. Baker, his teacher).

↓

Plot:	I gave Kevin a note in a sealed envelope to take to his mom, Mrs. Foster. Kevin thought the note contained news about his lack of effort in completing math homework on time. I have tried several techniques in class to encourage his homework completion, but none have been successful. I do not know what to try next to encourage him to complete his homework.

↓

Crisis/Climax:	Kevin hid the note in his backpack and did not plan to give it to his mom. While looking for a pencil to write a grocery list, Mrs. Foster found the envelope addressed to her. When Kevin saw his mom with the envelope, he hastily apologized to his mom about not completing his homework in math. Mrs. Foster was very upset about his hiding the note and his lack of effort in homework completion.

↓

Outcome:	Kevin confessed he hid the note because he did not complete his last homework assignments. The note from me to Mrs. Foster was asking her to be the chair for the PTO fund-raiser. Mrs. Foster telephoned me to accept the position and to discuss Kevin's homework. She was very concerned about Kevin's lack of effort in math and grounded Kevin for hiding the note and not completing his homework.

↓

Desired Outcome:	Kevin is working to complete his homework on time to remove the grounding punishment. Mrs. Foster and I are working together now to ensure Kevin is doing his homework by sending his graded homework from school on Thursdays. The homework is to be sent back on Fridays, signed by Mrs. Foster that she saw the graded work. I have learned a new technique to work with parents when students are not doing well in their homework.

outcome might be improved in the future. Mr. Baker reconstructed the reflective event, especially noticing the connection and relationships by plainly documenting the steps of all the different elements of setting, characters, plot, crisis/climax, outcome, and desired outcome. The flowchart clearly depicted the impact of the characters' actions on the outcome within the environmental setting.

Pause to Think . . .

Consider the suggestions for composing a reflective graphic organizer. What are your reactions to this reflective activity? Are there elements that might cause you difficulty to complete? If so, how could you overcome this problem?

All four of these supportive activities (double-entry journal, dialogue reflective journal, visual metaphors, and reflective graphic organizers), meet the motivational characteristics of being interesting, engaging, and challenging. Each activity *framed and reframed* reflective thought to concentrate on different aspects of the targeted problem, dilemma, event, or situation. Opportunities were presented for professionals to ask questions, seek answers, explore and clarify unfamiliar concepts, and share knowledge within the context of reflective activities. Reflection was explored and analyzed from different perspectives, resulting in individuals moving further along the journey toward more insightful reflective thought.

CHAPTER SUMMARY

When novice individuals approach reflective practice, their developmental experiences, skills, and abilities vary. Individuals typically do not progress in their understanding and skill of reflective thought without instruction and practice in reflective thinking. For individuals to become more effective reflective practitioners, instructors must provide the instruction and opportunities individuals need to begin their journey as well as continuing support all along the way.

Various supportive and structured activities were deliberately designed for individuals to examine alternative interpretations that promote critical thinking about self and situation, experiences, and dilemmas. Each of the supportive activities provide opportunities for reasoning, evaluation of intuitive beliefs, and exploration of individual perspectives. By experiencing these varied formats, individuals are challenged and reflective thought is promoted with continuous professional opportunities.

CHAPTER STUDY QUESTIONS

After reading this chapter, use these questions to discuss with your colleagues:

1. Based on personal experiences, what strategies have you used to improve reflective thought?
2. After reading about different reflective formats in this chapter, what new insights into the presented benefits and weaknesses have you discovered from the various strategies?
3. How is reflection considered a developmental process over time, rather than an instantaneous product *on the spot*?
4. Explain Ross's theory of *reframing* an event, situation, or dilemma for reflection.
5. Compare the double-entry journal to the dialogue reflective journal. Tell two ways they are different.

PROBLEM SETS/ACTIVITIES

1. Working individually, follow the directions previously provided in the text for this problem set/activity. You will need paper and pencil for the activities. If available, computers also can be used.
   Choose from the two supportive formats of writing using a matrix: double-entry journal or dialogue reflective journal. Recall an event, situation, or dilemma to use in reflection and complete the journal entry. (Each individual then will share the journal entry with the group.)
2. Working individually, follow the directions previously provided in the text for a collage construction. You will need paper, pencil, magazines, newspaper, glue, and backing paper for the activities or computers and clip art.
   Recall an event, situation, or dilemma different from the one used in question 1 to complete this activity. Use the directions to complete the collage, along with the script. Share the graphic with the whole group.
3. Construct a reflective graphic organizer, using the directions provided in the text.

Recall an event, situation, or dilemma different from those used in questions 1 or 2 to complete this activity. Use the directions to complete the graphic organizer, along with the script. Share with the whole group.
4. Compare and contrast the three different reflective formats just completed.

Which of the formats helped you the most in your journey toward more effective reflective thought? Why did you choose that format? (This activity can be completed orally in the group or as an individually written assignment or a combination. Use paper and pencil if needed.)

BIBLIOGRAPHY

Archambault, R. D. (1974). *John Dewey on education: Selected writings.* Chicago: University of Chicago Press.

Baird, J. R., Fensham, P. J., Gunstone, R. F., & White, R. T. (1991). *A study of the importance of reflection for improving science teaching and learning.* National Association for Research in Science Teaching. New York: John Wiley and Sons.

Bakhtin, M. (1981). *The dialogic imagination: Four essays.* Austin: University of Texas Press.

Callister, L. C. (1993). The use of student journals in nursing education: Making meaning out of clinical experience. *Journal of Nursing Education, 32,* 185–186.

Cowan, J., & Westwood, J. (2006). Collaborative and reflective professional development. *Active Learning in Higher Education, 7*(1), 63–71.

Dewey, J. (1933). *How we think: A restatement of the relation of reflective thinking to the educative process.* Boston: Houghton Mifflin.

Dyment, J. E., & O'Connell, T. S. (2003). *Journal writing in experiential education: Possibilities, problems, and recommendations.* (ERIC Document Reproduction Service No. ED479358).

Edgar, I. R. (2004). *Guide to imagework: Imagination-based research methods.* New York: Routledge.

Greiman, B. C., & Covington, H. K. (2007). Reflective thinking and journal writing: Examining student teachers' perceptions of preferred reflective modality, journal writing outcomes, and journal structure. *Career and Technical Education Research, 32*(2), 115–139. Retrieved July 13, 2008 at http://scholar.lib.vt.edu/ejournals/CTER/v32n2/pdf/greiman.html.

Heinrich, K. T. (1992). The intimate dialogue: Journal writing by students. *Nurse Educator, 17*(6), 17–21.

Hill, R. (2005). Reflection as a professional development strategy during organizational change. *Reflective Practice, 6,* 213–220.

Hollister, B. C. (2000). *Reflective thinking, John Dewey, and PBL.* Retrieved July 13, 2008 http://www.imsa.edu/center/bernie/html/dewey.html.

Killion, J. P., & Todnem, G. R. (1991). A process for personal theory building. *Educational Leadership, 48*(6), 14–16.

Lai, G., & Calandra, B. (2007). Using online scaffolds to enhance preservice teachers' reflective journal writing: A qualitative analysis. *International Journal of Technology in Teaching and Learning, 3*(3), 66–81.

McDermott, J. (Ed.). (1973). *The philosophy of John Dewey* (Vols. 1–2). New York: G. P. Putnam's Sons.

McIntosh, P., & Webb, C. (2006). *Creativity and reflection: An approach to reflexivity in practice.* Retrieved June 16, 2009 from http://www.leeds.ac.uk/medicine/meu/lifelong06/papers/P_PaulMcIntosh.pdf.

Mezirow, J., Brookfield, S., Candy, P. C., Deshler, D., Dominice, P. F., Gould, R. L., et al. (1990). *Fostering critical reflection in adulthood.* San Francisco: Jossey-Bass.

Pedro, J. Y. (2005). Reflection in teacher education: Exploring pre-service teachers' meanings of reflective practice. *Reflective Practice, 6,* 49–66.

Risko, V. J., Roskos, K., & Vukelich, C. (2002). Prospective teachers' reflection: Strategies, qualities, and perceptions in learning to teach reading. *Reading Research and Instruction, 41*(2), 149–176.

Ross, D. (1989). First steps in developing a reflective approach. *Journal of Teacher Education, 40*(2), 22–30.

Ross, D. (1990). Programmatic structures for the preparation of reflective teachers. In R. T. Clift, W. R. Houston, & M. C. Pugach (Eds.), *Encouraging reflective practice in education* (pp. 97–118). New York: Teachers College Press.

Schön, D. (1983). *The reflective practioner: How professionals think in action.* New York: Basic Books.

Schön, D. A. (1987). *Educating the reflective practitioner: Toward a new design for teaching and learning in the professions.* San Francisco: Jossey-Bass.

van Manen, M. (1991). *The tact of teaching: The meaning of pedagogical thoughtfulness.* Albany, NY: SUNY Press.

Webb, P. T. (1999, February). *The use of language in reflective teaching: Implications for self-understanding.* Paper presented at the annual meeting of the American Association of Colleges for Teacher Education, Washington, DC.

Chapter Three

Becoming Critically Reflective

> Reflection is the ability to stand apart from the self, and to critically ex-
> amine one's actions and the context of those actions for the purpose of
> a consciously driven mode of professional activity (Berlack & Berlack,
> 1981, p. 3).

OVERVIEW

Reflecting on significant episodes in professional practice is essential to the
development of professional judgment. Unless reflection involves some form
of challenge and critique of professional values, it tends to simply reinforce
existing patterns and tendencies. Individuals must change their cognitive
awareness to deliberately shift perspectives of their practice. To develop
professional judgments, individuals have to move beyond typical habits of
thought to critical reflection. In this chapter, the use of classroom scenarios
as the catalyst for analyzing reflective thought is highlighted.

CRITICAL REFLECTION AS REFLECTIVE THOUGHT

Critical reflection is composed of personal discourse of reasons for decisions
about events, taking into consideration the broader contexts of historical,
social, and political considerations. Critical reflection, as defined by Cranton
(1996), is the process by which individuals:

- identify the assumptions governing their actions.
- locate the historical and cultural origins of these assumptions.

- question the meaning of the assumptions.
- develop alternative ways of acting (as cited in Stein, 2009).

How does critical reflection differ from thoughtful reflection previously discussed in chapters 1 and 2? Willis (1999) described a process of three stages involved in critical reflection: dispositional, contextual, and experiential (as cited in Stein, 2009).

1. Dispositional reflection was characterized as being composed of personal (a) values, (b) preferences, and (c) characteristics of the person engaged in reflection.
2. Contextual reflection was composed of cultural forces, such as race, gender, ethnicity, institutional policies, and personal knowledge and skills that have the potential to shape the event.
3. Experiential reflection focused on thoughts and feelings that occurred from revisiting the event either in thought, verbally, or in writing.

Pause to Think . . .

Identify a critical incident in your life.

Using Cranton's four processes, relate them to your critical dilemma.

CRITICAL INCIDENTS: A VENUE FOR CRITICAL REFLECTION

Critical incidents, advocated by Tripp (1993), are venues for teaching critical reflection. A critical incident is an interpretation of a significant episode in a particular context rather than a routine occurrence. Typically, a critical incident is personal to an individual. Incidents only become critical, that is problematic, if the individual sees them in this way. Reflecting on an incident after the incident has taken place is when it is defined as critical. The incident becomes critical because it causes an individual to pause and take note. For example, two teachers. Ms. Mitchell and Ms. Williams, are in the classroom discussing a message from the principal. They both observe one student who gets out of his seat several times to sharpen his pencil. This is a routine occurrence that happens many times during a school day. Ms. Mitchell observes this incident, but thinks no more about it. Ms. Williams referred back to the incident several times during the day, because she was aware that no children were to be out of their seats, and she was struggling to establish a consistent classroom routine with her students, and especially this student. For Ms. Mitchell, the incident was not critical, but for Ms. Williams, the incident was critical. Interpreting the incident as critical motivated Ms. Williams to analyze the incident to determine the most effective way to establish classroom routines.

Critical incident analysis is an approach to dealing with challenges in everyday practice. For example, a critical incident could be students talking when other students are presenting their ideas or students who constantly arrive late for a class. As reflective practitioners, individuals need to pose questions about practice, refusing to accept *what is*. Individuals need to explore situations that occur in day-to-day work in order to understand these incidents better and find alternative ways of reacting and responding to them.

Thuynsma (2001) defined a critical incident as a turning point that results in changes in the perceptions of effectiveness or success. These characteristics influence the quality of reflection and the criteria individuals use to evaluate their decisions. A critical incident is systematically analyzed by using the following process:

1. Identify the critical incident.
2. Describe the contextual background leading to the incident.
3. Isolate the incident by visualizing the episode.
4. State the critical incident in question format (Use the five Ws: who, what, when, where, why).
5. Recognize personal point of view or possible bias.
6. Gather all evidence relevant to the incident.
7. Make inferences regarding why the incident occurred.
8. Draw conclusions based on all evidence and inferences.
9. Evaluate for future actions.
10. Plan and transfer for usage to professional repertoire.

Pause to Think . . .

Use your critical incident from the Pause to Think activity box above.

Use the first five steps above to systematically analyze your critical incident.

Using a Venn diagram, compare and contrast your responses from this activity and the previous Pause to Think activity.

ANALYSIS: A TOOL FOR CRITICAL REFLECTION

Analysis of critical incidents enables an individual to examine all aspects of an episode and determine multiple perspectives. Ross and Bondy (1996) defined reflective teaching as making rational and ethical choices about what and how to teach and assuming responsibility for those choices. Rodriquez and Sjostrom (1998) concluded that individuals should possess the following characteristics for reflective teaching:

- Recognize cognitive and social importance of learning.
- Value the role of the learner in constructing meaning.
- View learning from multiple perspectives.
- Utilize knowledge of the learners' backgrounds and experiences.

Tripp (1993) noted that the analysis of a critical incident tends to produce an approach to classroom teaching (or professional judgment) that can be termed *interpretative*. He stated, "This term [interpretative] is to emphasize that professional judgment is based upon analysis of our ideas of the meaning of the incidents rather than on our experience of the incidents themselves" (p. 28). In fact, interpretation is essential to professional practice because it always comes between observation and action. For example, a young student teacher, Mr. Johnson, observed two students who appeared to be cheating on an exam. Although Mr. Johnson knew that cheating was not permissible, he interpreted the event to have moral and ethical implications for the students involved based on his own moral code.

In this case about cheating, the student teacher responded to the students' actions through two interpretative lenses. One lens was focused on the classroom policy. The other lens was focused on the moral and ethical implications of the action. In the final analysis, the student teacher examined the incident from more than one perspective in order to determine the best course of action.

Pause to Think . . .

Assume you are a teacher and you observed a student sleeping in class.

In a small group, describe your interpretation of this event and how you would react.

Discuss the underlying reasons regarding why you reacted as you did.

PROFESSIONAL LEARNING COMMUNITIES

Brookfield (1995) suggested that reflective groups, such as Professional Learning Communities (PLCs), as mentioned in chapter 1, could be quite useful for critical reflection discussions. One way to begin a critical reflection discussion is to use a critical incident as a *springboard* for thought. Brookfield recommended structuring the conversations with three different roles: storyteller, detective(s), and umpire. These three groupings form a triad to discuss the critical incident, with each individual in the triad taking on a unique role.

The storyteller frames the conversation of the event. This person recounts the incident that includes the context, the people involved, and the critical incident. The storyteller is typically the primary person involved. This individual describes the incident through his/her perspectives, including resolutions and outcomes. The storyteller recants reflective thought.

The detective(s) asks critical questions related to the event. The role of the detective is to ask those probing questions that force the storyteller to clarify personal values, beliefs, cultural forces, or individual feelings that possibly shaped the interpretation of the event. The detective(s) frame the event into different or varied contexts and ask *what, why,* and *how* questions to elicit critical reflective thought. The questions are structured and related to the forces and characteristics found in Willis's (1999) three stages of critical reflection, namely:

- Dispositional: An example of a question related to a dispositional reflection is, "What do you believe about . . ."
- Contextual: An example of a question related to a contextual reflection is, "Why do you think . . ."
- Experiential: An example of a question related to an experiential reflection is "How do you feel about . . ."

The umpire oversees the process to maintain the focus on the task. Critical reflective discussions have the potential to be caustic, focusing on personalities of the group rather than remaining objective with feelings detached. The umpire is perhaps the most difficult role of the triad because remaining detached when personal feelings are involved may lead to dissension in the group.

Pause to Think . . .

Refer back to the pervious scenario of the fifth-grade students caught cheating on an exam.

In your own words, ad-lib to expand the details of the scenario.

In a group of three persons, take on the role of storyteller, detective, and umpire.

Discuss in your group of three how you felt taking on your individual role.

Was it difficult or easy? What could have made the role easier for you?

Case Study Technique

Brookfield (1995), a university professor, used a different technique to generate critical reflection. He developed the Critical Incident Questionnaire and used it weekly with his students. He adapted the case study technique with his university undergraduate students as a way to collect data and improve his teaching style and instructional decision making. He asked his students to reflect on his teaching to raise his awareness of dispositional, contextual, or experiential elements used in his teaching.

The classroom was composed of a diverse population, and he wanted to insure his personal feelings, bias, and values were not evident in his teaching. The results of his questionnaire provided immediate critical feedback on a weekly basis. Brookfield was able to monitor and adjust his repertoire of strategies based on this feedback. The Critical Incident Questionnaire required students to designate particular learning activities that were most:

1. engaging
2. distracting
3. surprising
4. confusing
5. affirming

This collective class reflection then provided Brookfield with a case study that supplied formative data for structuring his teaching activities for the following week. This activity could easily be adapted for use in Professional Learning Communities.

CRITICAL INCIDENT ANALYSIS: A CASE STUDY

Critical incident analysis involves reflecting on what has occurred. Unless reflection involves some form of challenge to and critique of professional values, patterns tend to simply reinforce existing habits and tendencies. Reflection is informed by a view of the world that is created by culture, values, and experiences.

Individuals must change awareness through deliberately setting out to view the world of professional practice in new ways (Schön, 1987; Tripp, 1993). In other words, to develop professional judgment, individuals have to move beyond common ways of interpreting situations. Interpretation of critical incidents provides insight into individuals' ways of knowing and reflecting.

The following section provides a case study with examples of critical incident analysis *(Critical Incident Analysis, 2009)*. This method is portrayed in the following case study that represents detailed reflections on significant incidents in teaching. The case study showcases dispositional, contextual, and experiential elements within a teaching episode.

CASE STUDY: STUDENT'S WORK CHRONICALLY LATE

Background of the Incident

Jeremy, a student in Ms. Patel's English class, failed to submit a research paper on time. Jeremy came to class and asked for an extension for the paper because he had been sick. Ms. Patel agreed he could hand it in to her by next Thursday. However, he failed to attend the class the following week; no contact had been made and no one had heard from him. When Jeremy finally returned and was asked why he had not handed in the paper, he said that it would be ready the next day. Jeremy said he had been sick and had asked a friend to proofread his work. His friend told him that his paper had a lot of mistakes.

Ms. Patel was unsure how to handle the situation. Jeremy usually attended class regularly, contributed to class discussions, and submitted work on time. However, in this situation Jeremy failed to turn work in on time and did not offer reasons for his nonsubmission or his absence. These behaviors were strange and atypical.

Once Jeremy returned to school, Ms. Patel made an appointment to meet with him to discuss his late work. Ms. Patel explained that his behavior was annoying and disturbing because it was not typical and he had failed to provide any rationale for his late paper. Ms. Patel reminded Jeremy that there was a school policy about the consequences of late work. Jeremy was apologetic but seemed unaware that school policy allowed deducting points from late work each day without a doctor's excuse.

Teacher's Reflections from the Previous Scenario

This incident stood out for me because it may show difficulties in my teaching style. I may have been too relaxed and informal. I wanted to put students at ease and promote discussion in class. My easygoing nature may have led to some students taking advantage of my relaxed and nonconfrontational manner.

The situation of the classroom on this particular day may have influenced the student's behavior. I was distracted by several groups of students who needed my attention. One group of students needed my assistance and were talking to each other, while others were trying to engage me in their conversation. Also, other students in the classroom were asking me, and each other, unrelated questions as a result of my informal style.

I think past experience affected the way I handled this situation as I had essentially let the student *off the hook*. Letting this student off the hook was due, in part, to my assessment of his individual character, which I had based on previous experiences with the student. Although frustrated, I wanted to avoid any impulsive or drastic actions.

I rationalized that the student may have forgotten the consequences of not submitting work and that I had not been consistent in reminding the students of the consequences. Jeremy had attempted to complete the essay and gain feedback from his friend, suggesting he wanted to submit the best work possible.

Teacher Insight and Learning Points

It seems extreme to go to the student and discuss the event again, but this episode will change my future actions. Through reflection I learned the importance of:

- reinforcing school policies and procedures in my classroom
- reminding students of requirements for the assignment
- communicating clearly and consistently
- clarifying personal feelings, bias affecting my decisions, and their effect on my decisions.

Case Study Analysis

Analyzing Ms. Patel's response to the critical incident involving Jeremy's homework assignment, the three elements of dispositional, contextual, and experiential are evident. Dispositional reflection is apparent in her statement of personal values. She described her informal and relaxed teaching style and her nonconfrontational classroom management, which are prime examples of preference and values. This teaching style creates conflicting forces between Ms. Patel's personal values (dispositional) and school policies (contextual).

Even though Ms. Patel knew the policy of late assignments, she reverted to personal preferences regarding this student. In the past, this particular student had met Ms. Patel's expectations and caused her to have positive feelings toward him. The importance of upholding school policies was not a driving force in her decision-making process.

Pause to Think . . .

Put yourself *in the shoes* of Ms. Patel. Think of a time when you disregarded policies and let personal feelings influence your actions.

Write your response by describing the incident, including your reactions.

Discuss your response with a partner.

CHAPTER SUMMARY

The characteristics of mature reflective judgment indicate that individuals also must develop the ability to view situations from multiple perspectives. This ability to search for alternative explanations of events and use evidence in supporting or evaluating a decision is hinged on effective critical reflection. Critical reflection can help individuals confront and challenge their worldview and assist them in learning how these beliefs affect their professional decision making.

Analyzing critical incidents is one approach in the process of critical reflection. Critical incident analysis enables close examination of all aspects of an episode in order to determine the best course of action. Professional Learning Communities aid the process of critical reflection through dialogue in a supportive environment. There are three stages of critical reflection, namely:

- dispositional
- contextual
- experiential

A storyteller, a detective, and an umpire facilitate each stage of the critical reflection process. The storyteller is one who describes the context of the critical incident. The detective is one who asks probing questions that cause individuals to think deeply about the incident, and the umpire is the one who oversees the process by maintaining an objective focus.

CHAPTER STUDY QUESTIONS

After reading this chapter, use these study questions to discuss with your peers.

1. Describe the three roles of the critical reflection discussion as defined in this chapter by Brookfield.
2. What is a critical incident, and how does critical incident analysis promote critical reflection?
3. What are the three stages of critical reflection?
4. What is a Professional Learning Community, and how do Professional Learning Communities promote reflective practice?
5. What strategy can be used to promote discussion in a Professional Learning Community?

PROBLEM SETS/ACTIVITIES

1. Working in a small group of three to four peers, brainstorm possible critical incidents you have experienced. As a group, select one of the incidents for completing the activities below. Use a large piece of paper that can be displayed in the room (post-it easel pad) to record the selected critical incident and your responses to the following points. Display and share your responses with the whole group.
   Activities to complete:

   - Isolate the incident by visualizing the episode.
   - Identify the critical incident.
   - Describe the contextual background leading to the incident.
   - State the critical incident in question format (Use the five Ws: who, what, when, where, why).

2. Individually, read the case study below and complete the bulleted activities. Record your answers and be ready to share.

   - Find the critical incident in the case study below.
   - Identify and describe the personal point of view or possible bias.
   - Record all evidence relevant to the personal point of view or bias.
   - Make interpretative inferences as to the meaning of the incident.
   - Describe the dispositional, contextual, and experiential elements in the case study.
   - Draw conclusions based on all evidence and inferences.

Case Study: Poor School Performance

Two ninth-grade teachers, Ms. Rodriquez and Mr. Farley, were meeting to discuss the work of one of their students, Colby. Ms. Rodriquez commented that Colby's work did not meet her expectations and was not typical of him. She considered Colby a good student. Ms. Rodriquez told Mr. Farley that Colby was friends with Lu and Mario, who she considered a couple of *lazy boys*, and he was beginning to take on their traits and bad habits.

Mr. Farley didn't think there would be any point in saying anything to Colby. After thinking about Colby's well-being, Ms. Rodriquez decided that if Mr. Farley had no apparent interest in Colby's achievement, then she was going to take some action. She decided to speak privately to Colby after English class about his work, the upcoming term paper, and his choice of friends. The next morning after class, Ms. Rodriquez asked Colby to stay after class so she could speak to him. "Colby, I am very concerned about your lack of effort recently. I noticed that you have been hanging around with Lu and Mario. You do realize that you are identified by the company you keep, don't you? I would hate to see your work and your appearance take a turn for the worse. You know that you have a lot of talent in writing, and I can see bright things in your future." Colby shrugged his shoulders, rolled his eyes, and walked off.

The next morning the semester term papers were due in Ms. Rodriquez's English class. The night before, Colby, Lu, and Mario frantically searched the Internet for papers on the assigned topic. The three boys each decided to take a paper from the Internet, make some minor changes, and turn them in as their own work.

When Ms. Rodriquez began to grade the paper, she immediately saw that Colby, Lu, and Mario's papers were very similar except for a few words. Ms. Rodriquez was frustrated. Her talk to Colby had no effect, and she realized that Lu and Mario had a strong negative influence on Colby. Ms. Rodriquez was left with a huge knot in her stomach knowing that severe action had to be taken.

BIBLIOGRAPHY

Berlack, A., & Berlack, H. (1981). *Dilemmas of schooling: Teaching and social change.* New York: Methuen.

Brookfield, S. D. (1995). *Becoming a critically reflective teacher.* San Francisco: Jossey-Bass.

Cranton, P. (1996). *Professional development as transformative learning: New perspectives for teachers of adults.* San Francisco: Jossey-Bass.

Critical Incident Analysis. (2009). Retrieved September 24, 2009, from http://legacy-www.coventry.ac.uk/legacy/_ched/research/critical.htm.

Dewey, J. (1933). *How we think: A restatement of the relation of reflective thinking to the educative process.* Boston: Heath.

Haddock, J. (1997). Reflection in groups: Contextual and theoretical considerations within nurse education and practice. *Nurse Education Today, 17*(5), 381–385.

Hatton, N., & Smith, D. (1995). *Reflection in teacher education: Towards definition and implementation.* The University of Sydney: School of Teaching and Curriculum Studies.

Kember, D. (1999). Determining the level of reflective thinking from students' written journals using a coding scheme based on the works of Mezirow. *International Journal of Lifelong Education, 18*(1), 18–30.

King, R. M., & Hibbison, E. P. (2000). *The importance of critical reflection in college teaching: Two reviews of Stephen Brookfield's book*, Becoming a critically reflective teacher. *Inquiry, 5*(2). Retrieved September 24, 2009 from http://www.vccaedu.org/inquiry/inquiryfall2000/i-52-king.html.

Peterson, B. R. (2007). The characterization of reflection by student teachers using the critical incident technique. *Dissertation Abstracts International, 69*(02), August 2008. (UMI No. 3301645).

Richards, J. C., & Lockhart, C. (1994). *Reflective teaching in second language classrooms.* Cambridge: Cambridge University Press.

Rodriquez, Y., & Sjostrom, B. (1998). Critical reflection for professional development: A comparative study of nontraditional adult and traditional student teachers. *Journal of Teacher Education, 4*(3), 177–186.

Ross, D., & Bondy, E. (1996). The continuing reform of a university teacher education program: A case study. In K. Zeichner, S. Melnick, and M. Gomez (Eds.), *Currents of reform in preservice teacher education* (pp. 62–79). New York: Columbia University Teachers College Press.

Schön, D. A. (1987). *Educating the reflective practitioner: Toward a new design for teaching and learning in the professions.* San Francisco: Jossey-Bass.

Stein, D. (2009). Teaching critical reflection. Retrieved September 24, 2009 from http://www.inspiredliving.com/business/reflection.htm.

Thuynsma, B. (2001). *Caring in teaching: Critical incidents in preservice teachers' field experiences that influence their career socialization.* Unpublished dissertation, State University of New York at Albany.

Tripp, D. (1993). *Critical incidents in teaching: Developing professional judgment.* New York: Routledge.

Willis, P. (1999). Looking for what it's really like: Phenomenology in reflective practice. *Studies in Continuing Education, 21*(1), 91–112.

Chapter Four

Reflection Using the Emerging Technologies

The business of reflection in determining the true good cannot be done once and for all. . . . It needs to be done, and done over and over and over again, in terms of the conditions of concrete situations as they arise. In short, the need for reflection and insight is perpetually recurring (Dewey, 1932, p. 231).

OVERVIEW

In the preceding three chapters, actions are described that individuals can use to become more reflective in their practice. There are certain concrete conditions that hinder this process. The content of this chapter addresses alternative approaches to reflection that will help individuals examine and better understand the nature of the reflective process within today's technological environment.

As the philosopher John Dewey noted in 1932, there is a need to perpetually reflect. A formidable challenge of accomplishing that goal is to reach individuals in their most comfortable, expressive mode. In this chapter, the purpose is to present a different kind of communication media called *emerging literacies* and explain how they can successfully be used to achieve a higher degree of reflection. In attempting to define literacies of the emerging technologies, it appears there is no one clear definition, perhaps because many more new literacies are constantly emerging, i.e., twitters, blikis, webinars, podcasts, vodcasts, and so on. The focus will be confined to the two powerful literacies of blogs and wikis that lend themselves well for integration within the reflective process. These two literacies are very popular and are quickly becoming the preferred communication media of choice.

EMERGING TECHNOLOGIES AS TOOLS FOR REFLECTION

To begin the discussion of emerging literacies, the typical definition of literacy needs to be expanded. If the underlying premise of literacy is for communication purposes, individuals need to become more aware of the rapid and far-reaching growth of technological tools of communication. Most educators who are familiar with the new literacies conclude that these literacies improve our ability to narrowly focus our thoughts, locate information, critique and analyze that information, summarize and synthesize our findings, and relay that information to others.

Because new literacies are constantly emerging, the focus of this chapter will be confined to two of these Internet publishing tools for integration within the reflective process, namely blogs and wikis. These emerging technologies have the capacity to change the very nature of the reflective process, which was once predominantly paper text. Because of their ease of use and quick visual availability, these two emerging literacies offer many of the features sought by professionals for effective reflection.

Even our sources for information have changed from hard copy reference books to online sources to find current technology terms and information. Merriam-Webster Online Dictionary (www.merriam-webster.com/dictionary), Wikipedia (www.wikipedia.org), and Webopedia (www.webopedia.com) are examples of sites that have become the Internet technological information sources of choice for many professionals.

BLOGS: AN OVERVIEW AND APPLICATION TO PRACTICE

Definition and Use of Blogs

On Wikipedia a blog (a contraction of web log) is defined as a website of regularly written entries of various comments, which may be in response to what someone else wrote or a comment on a new subject not yet addressed (http://wikipedia.org). Graphics, such as clip art, hyperlinks to other Internet sites, or even video can be added in a blog. An important part of blogs is the social interaction among readers who reply to others' postings.

While blogs originally began as individual and isolated personal journal entries on the web, they now are recognized as interactive and collaborative in nature. Some see blogs as a new social and professional network. Probably most individuals are familiar with the social networking sites of MySpace and Facebook or have possibly used a discussion board. One major way blogging differs from online discussion postings within a university course is that blogs are posted and open to the Internet world that virtually millions of people read and respond to. Ideas, comments, and feedback spread quickly through blogs. This open blogging access presents some potential problems for the blogger (person who blogs). Those beginning to blog should be aware that blogs are a public forum; therefore, people should not post private information to a blog.

Characteristics of Blogs

One of the strongest advantages of using blogs as a reflective mode is the immediate feedback received by the participants. On the University of Wisconsin-Madison's webpages (as cited by Cain, 2008) a list of these characteristics of reflective feedback in blogs is presented as:

1. promoting reflection as part of a dialogue between the giver and receiver of feedback. Both parties are involved in observing, thinking, reporting, and responding.
2. focusing on observed behavior rather than on the person. Refers to what an individual does rather than to what we think s/he is.
3. being specific rather than general.
4. promoting reflection about strategies and the teachers' responses to a specific strategy.
5. being directed toward behavior that the receiver can change.
6. considering the needs of both the receiver and giver of feedback.
7. being solicited rather than imposed. Feedback is most useful when the receiver actively seeks feedback and is able to discuss it in a supportive environment.
8. being well timed. In general, feedback is most useful at the earliest opportunity after the given behavior.
9. involving sharing information rather than giving advice, leaving the individual free to change in accordance with personal goals and needs.
10. considering the amount of information the receiver can use rather than the amount the observer would like to give. Overloading an individual with feedback reduces the likelihood that the information will be used effectively.
11. requiring a supportive, confidential relationship built on trust, honesty, and genuine concern.

Pause to Think . . .

Read the following scenario and think back to a time when you were beginning a new position. Is Jennifer's reflection similar to one you have had? Was there someone with whom you could share your reflection?

Consider these blog entries of a first-year middle school teacher, Jennifer (J), and the feedback she received from an experienced teacher, Stephanie (S):

J: (October 11) I was really nervous today. I forgot to bring my seating chart to class with me. It sure would have helped because I am still trying to learn the students' names. I ran out of time again to do a review of the lesson. I did tell the students about the homework assignment, but I should have made sure they wrote it down. I really need to work on not forgetting details. Did anyone else have a bad day?

S: (October 12) This is my sixth year of teaching. It has taken me this long to feel like I'm capable (well at least most of the time, instead of never). You will get better at that detail thing. Try making a list or notes to yourself, see if that helps. I found it helps me be organized. Hang in there—we're all in this together.

In her short blog entry, Jennifer, a teacher, is seemingly more aware of problems concerning herself than concentrating on her students. Even this simple act of reflection, which appears shallow, can lay a foundation for deeper insight over time. She is soliciting feedback and help from others. Note the encouraging and timely feedback she receives from Stephanie, as well as the sharing of information. This example supports the research of F. Eide and B. Eide (2005), who found blogging has a positive impact on teacher involvement because it promotes more analytical thinking, elicits association of similar events, and encourages social interaction.

Stephanie helped Jennifer to remember that experience is going to be her best teacher in these small tasks on which she is focusing. She connected Jennifer's first-year experiences to her sixth-year confidence. Stephanie analyzed Jennifer's problem, offered a possible solution, and ended with encouragement.

The Research Base for Blogs

Although the use of blogs for reflection is relatively new, there are several studies in which it was found that blogging is an effective tool for integrating reflective processes. The age of bloggers does seems to influence the enjoyment and type of responses, as younger bloggers feel more comfortable in the blogging environment while older bloggers are somewhat more reluctant to express themselves. A probable reason is that the younger adults have used technology from childhood and are more comfortable using blogs and wikis. For some adults just learning the use of computers may make them feel uncomfortable when beginning to blog, but most professionals who use technology daily should not have a problem (see discussion in Bonk, Cummings, Hara, Fischler, & Lee, 2000; Bonk, Malikowski, Angeli, & East, 1998; Fiedler, 2003; Khourey-Bowers, 2005; Ray & Hocutt, 2006; Shoffner, 2005; Suzuki, 2004; West, Wright, & Graham, 2005).

GETTING STARTED WITH A BLOG

Setting up a blogging site is a relatively easy task. Three things to consider in choosing which blog site to use are:

1. Is the site free or is there a charge for use?
2. Does it have limited advertisements and pop-ups?
3. Does it contain inappropriate weblinks from the site?

Structuring the Blog

In beginning to investigate the social nature of blogs, professionals need to be aware of how to organize and structure the blogging site and how to plan learning opportunities for the bloggers that will best take advantage of these technological devices. One major challenge for the blog site organizer lies in knowing how to take individuals' knowledge, skills, and particular proficiencies and apply those to achieve higher levels of reflection. One practical way to begin reflective blogging is with specific and structured directions that teachers will feel comfortable using. Because blogging may be a new experience for some individuals, structured directions may reduce the potential stress and fearfulness of a new technology. Individuals then will be more at ease and willing to try this new experience when structured directions are provided.

Reflective Blogs for Experienced and Preservice Teachers

After reading a text or experiencing an event in the classroom, teachers are asked to reflect their thoughts (positive or negative) and beliefs that are related to that assigned reading or after experiencing the event. The posting can be very structured by the teacher or unstructured with a very broad prompt, such as "Share your thoughts about a classroom problem you experienced yesterday at Modern Middle School." However, very structured prompts are typically more successful for teachers who are novices in the reflective process.

Blogs invite professionals to explore the written discourse of learning communities—communities in which they learn together. The comments in the blog demonstrate that discourse is the context and substance, both process and product of beginning to learn to reflect.

In structuring the blogging experience, certain numbers of responses or contributions to the blog can be a requirement. To avoid the possibility of poor quality postings to the blog, some posting guidelines may be used.

Blog Guidelines for Blogging Novices

The following guidelines will aid in critical thinking, problem solving, content discussion, and experience sharing. These guidelines form directives for a very structured blog for novices. Instructors may want to modify guidelines as individuals become more experienced in blogging and when they are comfortable without this amount of structure. While working with teachers, one of the authors of this text constructed and used these guidelines for blogging:

1. Keep comments related to the main topic and add your thoughts, experiences, feelings, details, examples, and so forth. Do not simply agree or disagree. You need to add content to the discussion to demonstrate your reflection on knowledge of the assigned readings or classroom observations, supplemented with your personal experience.
2. Encourage interaction among others in your school, grade level, or department by reflecting on problem-solving opportunities and the questioning of self and others.
3. Use professional vocabulary and writing style throughout the blogging. For quality, any written work should be well written, free of spelling errors, and address the topics being discussed.
4. Use your initials plus a number for your posting signature, such as cm603 or a pseudonym plus a number, such as daydreamer630. Notify the blog's originator of your pseudonym.
5. Remember your posting is on a very public place. Do not use *any* specific names, specific places, school or department names, home addresses, e-mail address, or passwords. Pseudonyms always should be used if there is a need to place persons or places in context.
6. Notify the appropriate person if you receive any inappropriate comments to your postings.
7. Regular and active participation is essential!
8. It is essential that you read all the required material as well as the public discussion of the topics in the blog. Regular personal postings, as well as

immediate feedback to others about their postings, is essential to gain the most reflective experience from blogging.

Pause to Think . . .

Let's investigate some examples of blogs related to education. Choose a blog of your interest from the list and read the comments within the blog. Also note the weblinks to other educational blogs. Identify your blog choice and what impressed you about the blog.

http://budtheteacher.com/blog

http://www.thefacultyroom.org/

http://www.creativeliteracy.blogspot.com/

http://missrumphiuseffect.blogspot.com/

http://anne.teachesme.com/category/reflecting/

Summary Thoughts on Blogs

One of the most distinctive and worthwhile aspects of blogging is the ability to receive peer feedback and interact with others having similar purposes. Teachers develop problem-solving skills as their peer teachers share their experiences in blogs, particularly experiences that have caused them confusion or puzzlement. By reading each other's comments, teachers may interact and share how they have solved a similar problem in a similar situation. The blogger is assisted by the collaborative feedback, discussion, and other comments from those sharing common experiences. The collaborative comments and experiences help the blogger in clarifying personal beliefs, understandings, and plans for future action, which is such an important part of reflection. Effective reflection then leads to various types of change—whether change of thinking, change of beliefs, or change of actions.

Pause to Think . . .

Read the following scenario and make a mental or written note of any kind of change among our two middle school teachers (Stephanie and Jennifer) as they post to their blog.

> J: (October 14) Compared to Monday, I felt much more comfortable. I still felt a little nervous, but my confidence level was higher than last time. In regard to today's lesson, I feel everything went quite smoothly. As I mentioned in my last posting, my planning is not exactly the best. I tried making a list of stuff I needed to be sure I had before I left home. This was definitely helpful to me. It helped boost my confidence level and it also took my mind off whether or not I had everything. I still struggled with my time management. I only had left three minutes to make a closing. I did do better than on Monday; however, I would have liked to have had a few minutes more for my closing.
>
> S: (October 15) I appreciate your honesty and the feeling that you can share your experiences. We all grow through practice and through sharing problems or successes with others. We as teachers never get better by continuing to do things the "same old way." Trial and error, think again, and practice . . . and tomorrow we get to start fresh all over again.

Note that the novice teacher, Jennifer, is still concerned with herself and "how smoothly the class went." Her posting reveals some evidence of reflection, although weak. Stephanie is demonstrating a supportive attitude and they are starting a relationship built on trust, which is a result of the blogging. Can you imagine a new teacher being able to confide with an experienced teacher and receive such encouragement? Such is the strength of blogs—extremely strong problem-solving collaboration!

WIKIS: AN OVERVIEW AND APPLICATION TO PRACTICE

Definition and Use of Wikis

Another one of the powerful new Internet literacies is the wiki. Wiki derives its name from the Hawaiian word meaning *quick*. Probably the most familiar wiki is Wikipedia, the online encyclopedia. Wikis build on collaborative knowledge sharing, as Wikipedia so well demonstrates. Wikis offer a unique way to engage groups of students in collaborative ways while within a technological environment. The online discussion groups can truly be an anytime, anywhere, 24/7 environment.

A wiki can be viewed and edited by anyone with Internet access. This fact was perhaps the reason wikis were originally used for collaboration by technical engineers in developing software. The engineers could share and add knowledge within a quick and easily accessible environment.

Wikis possess a socially rich culture that contributes to powerful learning experiences and teacher autonomy. A new synergistic learning experience occurs in using a wiki, as teachers collaborate, negotiate, and share knowledge and opinions. Within this environment professionals learn to respect each other's opinions and ideas. The sense of audience within a wiki is very exciting because of this collaboration.

Lamb (2004) found wikis possess four attributes:

1. Anyone can change anything. (Anyone can typically rewrite, edit, or undo another's work.)
2. Wikis use simplified hypertext markup. (Tasks are simplified—very easy to use.)
3. WikiPageTitlesAreMashedTogether. (Space is saved, and linking to related pages is easier.)
4. Content is egoless, timeless, and never finished. (Wiki postings can be anonymous, open-ended, and can have several contributors to the postings.) (p. 36.)

Pause to Think . . .

Access the wiki site http://c2.com/cgi/wiki?TipsForBeginners.

Observe postings by groups. Access the OneMinuteWiki.

Make a note of the four attributes of wikis observed in these sites, as identified by Lamb (2004).

Benefits of Wikis

Summarizing the collaborative benefits to reflective practice, wikis provide opportunities to work in groups and create a feeling of community in a world where group efforts are quickly becoming the norm. Experienced and inexperienced professionals feel comfortable contributing in this nonthreatening environment.

Quality Issues

In the open environment where anyone can rewrite, edit, or undo work, some professionals are concerned about accuracy of content. Wiki content can be deleted or changed, but wikis also can have that content recovered. In addition, password-protected wikis are available for a closed environment of restricted wiki use.

Lack of Control over Copyright Issues

Some researchers are concerned with one person posting to a wiki and some-one else changing that person's postings. Who owns the copyright or text citations? This is a common concern. Davis (2007) lists four guidelines to ensure quality in wiki use:

1. Make use of the feature that alerts a wiki manager that changes have been made to the wiki. Check regularly to see what changes have been made and by whom.
2. Determine whether your wiki should be accessible to the public or be limited to a defined group.
3. Be aware of copyright and licensing issues when posting other people's work.
4. Emphasize "digital professionalism" to the community that can add content to, edit, or otherwise revise your wiki to remind users that it is a document many other people will see. Talk about and make clear what is, and is not, acceptable on the wiki (paragraphs 13–15).

GETTING STARTED WITH A WIKI

As with beginning blogs, wikis are also easy to create. Rather than individuals worrying about how to construct the site, the ease of creating the wiki allows them to concentrate on developing the content of the wiki.

Pause to Think . . .

When starting wiki use, begin at the website http://c2.com/cgi/wiki?WikiWikiSandbox with a practice area called a *sandbox* for individuals to work until they are more comfortable.

Use something like a get-acquainted activity, such as "If you could compare yourself to a plant, which would you be and why?" (Any fun writing activity that does not reveal identification of the wiki user is appropriate. The main purpose is to engage everyone and accustom them to posting in the wiki.) Rather than so many directions, consider encouraging individuals to ask each other for help in understanding the process of wiki use.

The value of wiki use for reflective practice, especially over time, has not been researched enough to be established. There are some situations, however, that wiki use positively impacts. In her studies of wiki pedagogy, Fountain (2005) concluded that wikis work best over time for problem solving, examining relationships of ideas, synthesizing and evaluating disciplines, questioning principles, responding to other's work, and learning to observe deeply without premature judgment.

Pause to Think . . .

Access two websites for examples of teachers using wikis for different purposes. One elementary school uses wikispaces for teachers to post homework assignments in a central location (information gathering and distributing). Access http://slehomework.wikispaces.com/slehomework to observe their efforts.

Another wikispace for teachers who want to improve their reading programs (more reflective practice here) is located at http://bookleads.wikispaces.com/message/view/home/4844127.

COMPARISON OF BLOGS AND WIKIS

Wikis, as well as blogs, do not require highly technical skills and thus, allow teachers to concentrate on information sharing and collaboration rather than learning difficult computer skills. Although both are communication tools of the new literacies, wikis differ from blogs in several ways. Blogs are much more structured than wikis; wikis are very flexible. Blogs are written in reverse chronological order, with the most current entry on top, whereas wikis can be structured many different ways, i.e., by category, by subject, and so on. Blogs are typically personal or professional postings while wikis are extremely collaborative. Teachers not only can write, edit, and publish for themselves in a wiki but also have the ability to rewrite, edit, and undo the work of other teachers. This ability in wikis to alter or undo the work of others in an open web environment is a concern for many people. Could this ability have led to the Wiki Prayer?

> Please, grant me the serenity to accept the pages I cannot edit,
> The courage to edit the pages I can,
> And the wisdom to know the difference.

> —Wiki Prayer
> (http://www.educause.edu/pub/er/erm04/erm0452.asp)

THE USE OF BLOGS AND WIKIS FOR IMPROVING REFLECTIVE PRACTICE

Someone may question the use of blogs and wikis in reflection. Perhaps the most compelling reason for use in reflection is their capacity to change the very nature of the reflective process, which was previously considered composing on paper or perhaps just mentally. The process of discourse by blogging is the context and process of reflecting in learning communities of teachers. Because of their ease of use and quick visual availability, blogs and wikis offer many advantages for effective reflection.

In their paper about wikis and blogs, McGee and Diaz (2007) identified the following characteristics of blogs and wikis that promote insightful reflection. Blogs and wikis are

1. communicative: to share ideas, information, and creations
2. collaborative: to work with others for a specific purpose in a shared work area
3. documentative: to collect and/or present evidence of experiences, thinking over time, productions, etc.
4. generative: to create something new that can be seen and/or used by others
5. interactive: to exchange information, ideas, resources, materials (p. 40).

Individuals may vary in their perceived views of reflection because of differing beliefs, values, concepts, and ways of thinking. Blogs and wikis provide a unique, new venue for teachers to share their ideas, opinions, and knowledge using this new media. Blogs and wikis have the capability to become the vehicles to connect theory and actual practice by transferring classroom actions into written thoughts.

Pause to Think . . .

Name several ways these new literacies of blogs and wikis offer professionals powerful communication and collaborative opportunities.

Because of the novel, social nature of blogs and wikis, certain individuals may enjoy this way to reflect more than other modes. Many professionals find this media of blogs and wikis far less threatening than other ways to reflect. By participating in varied modes of reflection, truly the right tool can be found for the right people at the right time.

With experience over time, all professionals generally become more fluent in reflective comments within blogs and wikis than in solitary written reflections. These professionals find suddenly they are involved as writers and readers in a continuing dialogue within a unique environment and thus create learning communities of interest. Because these new literacies are easy to use and, in most instances, free of charge this has contributed to their explosive use among various professionals.

CHAPTER SUMMARY

Teachers and other professionals should take advantage of these different venues in improving their reflective practice. The venues of new literacies are swiftly becoming the preferred communication tools of professionals because of their ease of use and availability. Instruction and individual work should be planned in purposeful reflective activities, using these new literacies of blogs and wikis. For example, individuals should be encouraged to use techniques in realistic situations, such as blogging with others about common experiences or events. Blogging helps users in being consciously aware of the processes and phases involved in reflection. The primary aim is to use these new tools to achieve more insightful reflection through the collaborative aspects of blogs and wikis. Through perpetual reflection, educators can regenerate and recreate themselves and their professional practice.

CHAPTER STUDY QUESTIONS

After reading this chapter, use these questions to discuss with your colleagues:

1. How should the definition of literacy be expanded to reflect the current use of literacy?
2. What specific characteristics of blogs and wikis enable these new emerging literacies to have such a major impact on developing more insightful reflection among users?
3. From your personal perspective, what are the possible advantages and possible disadvantages of reflective posting to a blog or wiki?

PROBLEM SETS/ACTIVITIES

Group participants into teams of three or four and follow the directions for the different problem sets/activities. You will need computer and Internet access, paper, and pencils for the activities.

1. Let's try blogging. There are several free servers for blogs, although some have a small charge. Explore these three examples and choose one to set up a blog:
   Blogger: http://www.blogger.com/start. This site is free and has clear directions to create a blog site in approximately five minutes.
   http://www.xanga.com/. Free basic service.
   http://teacherlingo.com. Free basic service.
2. Let's try some activities with wikis:
   For examples of wikis, access http://theconnectedclassroom.wikispaces. com/wikis and search this site for many educational wiki examples. Choose one example for this activity. Identify your wiki site, and using that wiki example, explain:
   • How are these wikis similar to blogs?
   • How does the use of these two new literacies allow teachers to read, synthesize information, and better problem solve while in a collaborative format?
3. Visit this website for suggestions to think about before you create a wiki:
   http://www.teachersfirst.com/content/wiki/wikiideas2.cfm.
   Take a wiki walk through some sample wikis for ideas!
   Then access these websites and choose one to create a wiki:
   http://www.editme.com/ (a demo site for wikis with a free trial offer)
   http://www.pbwiki.com (a free wiki site with password availability)
   http://www.jot.com (free wiki for up to five users, twenty pages, and passwords)
   http://www.wikispaces.com/site/for/teachers100K (free wiki space for K–12 teachers)

BIBLIOGRAPHY

Bonk, C. J., Cummings, J. A., Hara, N., Fischler, R., & Lee, S. M. (2000). A ten level web integration continuum for higher education: New resources, partners, courses, and markets. In B. Abbey (Ed.), *Instructional and cognitive impacts of web-based education* (pp. 56–77). Hershey, PA: Idea Group Publishing.

Bonk, C. J., Malikowski, S., Angeli, C., & East, J. (1998). Web-based case studies for preservice teacher education: Electronic discourse from the field. *Journal of Educational Computing, 19*(3), 269–306.

Boody, R. M. (1992). *An examination of the philosophic grounding of teacher reflection and one teacher's experience.* Unpublished doctoral dissertation. Provo, UT: Brigham Young University.

Boulos, M. N. K., Maramba, I., & Wheeler, S. (2005). *Wikis, blogs, and podcasts: A new generation of web-based tools for virtual collaborative clinical practice and education.* Retrieved July 22, 2008 from http://www.biomedcentral.com/1472-6920/6/41.

Bruster, B. (2008). *Reflective practice.* Retrieved August 12, 2008 from http://teacherlingo.com/blogs/nanner/archive/2008/02/12/reflective-practice.aspx.

Cain, M. A. (2008). *Peer consulting: Navigating the (sometimes) rocky shores of teaching and consulting.* Retrieved July 19, 2008 from http://speech.ipfw.edu/Peer-Review/reflections.html.

Davis, M. R. (2007). *Wiki wisdom: Lessons for educators.* Retrieved August 12, 2008 from http://www.edweek.org/dd/articles/2007/09/12/02wiki.h01.html.

Davison, R. (2008). Learning through blogging: Graduate student experiences. *eLearn Magazine.* Retrieved March 25, 2008 from http://www.elearnmag.org/subpage.cfm?section=best_practices&article=44-1.

Dewey, J. (1932). *The collected works of John Dewey, 1882–1953.* In J. A. Boydston (Ed.), *The later works* (LW 7:231). Carbondale and Edwardsville: Southern Illinois University Press.

Eide, F., & Eide, B. (2005, March 2). *Brain of the blogger.* In Eide Neurolearning Blog. Message posted to http://eideneurolearningblog.blogspot.com/2005/03/brain-of-blogger.html

Fiedler, S. (2003). Personal webpublishing as a reflective conversational tool for self-organized learning. In T. Burg (Ed.), *BlogTalks* (pp. 190–216). Vienna, Austria: Donau-Universität Krems.

Fountain, R. (2005). *Wiki pedagogy.* Retrieved August 11, 2008 from http://www.profetic.org:16080/dossiers/dossier_imprimer.php3?id_rubrique=110.

Hudson, L., & Glogoff, S. (2005). Extending instructional uses of blogs to the campus: A case study. *Technological Horizons in Education (THE).* Retrieved July 25, 2008 from http://download.101com.com/syllabus/conf/summer2005/PDFs/W15.pdf.

Khourey-Bowers, C. (2005). Emergent reflective dialogue among preservice teachers mediated through a virtual learning environment. *Journal of Computing in Teacher Education, 21*(4), 85–98.

Lamb, B. (2004). Wide open spaces: Wikis, ready or not. *EDUCAUSE Review (30)*5, 36–48.

Leu, D. J., Kinzer, C. K., Coio, J. L., & Cammack, D. W. (2004). *Toward a theory of new literacies emerging from the Internet and other information and communication technologies.* Retrieved July 22, 2008 from http://www.readingonline.org/newliteracies/leu/.

McGee, P., & Diaz, V. (2007). Wikis and podcasts and blogs! Oh, my! What is a faculty member supposed to do? *EDUCAUSE Review, 42*(5), 28–41.

Ray, B. B., & Hocutt, M. M. (2006). Teacher-created, teacher-centered weblogs: Perceptions and practices. *Journal of Computing in Teacher Education, 23*(1), 11–18.

Richardson, W. (2006). *Blogs, wikis, podcasts, and other powerful web tools for classrooms.* Thousand Oaks, CA: Corwin Press.

Shoffner, M. (2005). "If you write it down, you have to think about it": Incorporating weblogs into preservice teachers' reflective practice. In C. Crawford et al. (Eds.), *Proceedings of the Society for Information Technology and Teacher Education* (pp.

2095–2100). Chesapeake, VA: Association for the Advancement of Computing in Education.

Suzuki, R. (2004). Diaries as introspective research tools: From Ashton-Warner to blogs. *Teaching English as a Second or Foreign Language, 8*(1). Retrieved April 13, 2008 from http://www-writing.berkeley.edu/tesl-ej/ej29/int.html.

West, R. E., Wright, G. A., & Graham, C. R. (2005). Blogs, wikis, and aggregators: A new vocabulary for promoting reflection and collaboration in a preservice technology integration course. In C. Crawford et al. (Eds.), *Proceedings of the Society for Information Technology and Teacher Education* (pp. 1653–1658). Chesapeake, VA: Association for the Advancement of Computing in Education.

WEBLIOGRAPHY

Beyond The Four Walls. http://supportblogging.comLinks+to+School+ Bloggers

Blogger. http://www.blogger.com/start

Bud the Teacher. http://budtheteacher.com/blog

Creative Literacy. http://www.creativeliteracy.blogspot.com/

Edit Me. http://www.editme.com/

EduBlog Insights. http://anne.teachesme.com/category/reflecting/

The Faculty Room. http://www.thefacultyroom.org/

JotSpot Google. http://www.jot.com

Merriam-Webster Dictionary. http://www.merriam-webster.com/dictionary

The Miss Rumphius Effect. http://missrumphiuseffect.blogspot.com/

More Wiki Ideas. http://www.teachersfirst.com/content/wiki/wikiideas2.cfm

Peanut Butter Wiki. http://www.pbwiki.com

Teacher Lingo. http://teacherlingo.com

Webopedia. http://www.webopedia.com

Wiki prayer. http://www.educause.edu/pub/er/erm04/erm0452.asp

Wikipedia. http://www.wikipedia.com

Wikispaces. http://www.wikispaces.com/site/for/teachers100K

Xanga Blog Site. http://www.xanga.com/

Chapter Five

Language and Dialogue to Enhance Reflection

Thinking is an engagement of the mind that changes the mind.
(Heidegger, as cited in Costa & Kallick, 2008, p. 135).

OVERVIEW

The specific use of language and dialogue among professionals supports and influences reflective practice. Dialogue is a critical aspect of reflection and is used to deepen and shape the reflective process. This chapter is presented to support the use of the social processes of reflection and the elements of cognitive coaching to scaffold the reflective process.

Using techniques from cognitive coaching, individuals develop insights into reflection through introspective thinking, problem solving, and interactions with other professionals. Examples of specific cognitive coaching techniques and language are applied to reflection, enabling teachers the ability to use all aspects and levels of reflection, ultimately improving instructional practice and advancing student achievement.

REFLECTION AS A SOCIAL PROCESS

Examining the Greek origin helps with the understanding and interpretation of the word *dialogue*. The derivation of the word *dialogue* comes from the Greek word *dialogos. Dia* means "through" and *logos* is "the meaning of the word." Dialogue occurs between two people or many people. Dialogue occurs when meaning is flowing through and among individuals.

Using dialogue as a venue to deepen and enhance reflection occurs when a number of people are engaged in the reflective process. Dialogue is considered a natural form of speech and depends on mutual understandings, responses from others, and immediate feedback. For these reasons, dialogue is critical to the process of and the power in reflection.

Reflections are results of reflection-on-actions, thinking about previous actions, or possibly thinking on future actions as mentioned in a previous chapter. Naturally, individuals are deliberative thinkers; however, many times reflections remain internal and not voiced to others. At this point, actions may fall short of the optimum solutions possible.

Reflections that are internalized but not spoken are considered *inner speech*. Vygotsky (1986) referred to *inner speech* as "dynamic, unstable, and fluttering between words and thought and many times inner speech is disjointed, disconnected, and easily forgotten if not turned into spoken language" (p. 249). For example, individuals have daily situations that cause multiple opportunities for reflective thought. Internal questions arise, such as:

• What kind of action should be taken in this situation?
• What if the information were presented in a different manner?
• How should this problem be solved?

These examples of reflective thought are just some of many that remain internal.

Consider the repercussions if day after day reflective thoughts are not expressed to others and there are limited opportunities for reflective dialogue. Using dialogue with others to outwardly talk through reflective thoughts allows professionals to accept that the process is fluid with many aspects of uncertainty. Regardless of one's profession, reflective dialogue allows professionals to grow and develop in their practice.

Vygotsky (1978) stressed that the importance of interactions between learners, a novice and an expert, in a social environment results in the learning and development of both individuals involved. The teaching-learning process to which Vygotsky referred is the ongoing interaction of dialogue between the novice and the expert. Dewey (1933) contrasts reflective thinking with habits of thought, which are similar to inner thought. For example, *inner thought* remains in the mind and many times *what ifs* take over. These self-doubts are quickly followed by worry, anxiety, and uncertainty.

When inner thoughts are not verbalized and the elements of reflection ignored, individuals remain stagnant with thoughts, decision making abilities, and actions. Habits of thought are many times false and are based on premature assumptions. Therefore, thought and speech are two of the most important factors of human consciousness, resulting in changes in actions and beliefs.

LANGUAGE AND COMMUNICATION

Language and communication are at the heart of the reflective process. Language is the ideal example of a powerful negotiation tool, that when manipulated by others, can link the theory of development, knowledge, and instruction (Bruner, 1966). There is a direct causal link between the language teacher's use and the quality of his or her thinking.

Today, with the growing demands on teachers, reflection is necessary for ensuring quality decision making, professional growth, and adjustment to the ever-changing demands of the profession; thus, the need for reflection is ever increasing. Student achievement, diverse student needs, student motivation, and professional development are all critical elements for success. Teachers must infuse effective reflection into their daily routines to ensure these demands are met.

Teacher reflection must be ongoing and routinely practiced and enriched by collaborative efforts and dialogue with other professionals. Effective teachers spend time self-questioning, interacting with other professionals, and refining decisions that influence practice. They problem solve, refine inquiry, and explore options at various stages of the reflective process.

According to the research of Costa and Garmston (1994), there are five insights into human interactions, problem=solving, and information processing:

1. All behavior is rationally based on rather simple cognitive maps of reality.
2. When teachers talk about their reasons for doing things and respond to questions about their perceptions and teaching decisions, they often experience a sense of professional excitement.
3. Talking aloud about their thinking and decisions about teaching energizes and causes them to refine their cognitive maps and hence their instructional choices and behaviors.
4. Certain invisible, cognitive skills drive teaching and performance.
5. The visible cognitive skills can be categorized in four domains: preactive, interactive, reflective, and projective (p. 86).

Pause to Think . . .

Think about a time when you were engaged in a dialogue with someone else or a group of people. What were the results of the dialogue? How did you feel afterwards?

COGNITIVE COACHING TO INFLUENCE REFLECTION

Historically, cognitive coaching has been a vehicle for professional development and teacher collaboration. Costa and Garmston (1994) define cognitive coaching as a set of strategies to alter thinking and ultimately change professional practice. Providing teachers with mentors in a supportive learning environment allows teachers the opportunity to examine actions and to reflect on teaching and learning opportunities. Costa and Garmston reported that cognitive coaching has three primary goals:

- Building trust between the coach and the colleague
- Facilitating learning
- Enhancing professional growth

Cognitive coaching is an approach that generally pairs experienced *expert* teachers with *novice* teachers. The use of questioning techniques and dialogue from cognitive coaching enables teachers to incorporate problem solving and inquiry at a precise level. A close connection between a novice and an expert provides an environment of trust and respect, building essential communication skills.

The communication skills of questioning, reflecting, paraphrasing, probing, and summarizing enhance using precise language, and all are enhanced with cognitive coaching. An overwhelming body of research on cognitive coaching revealed that collaboration among professionals is one critical component to ensure continued professional growth (Edwards, 1995; Garmston, Linder, & Whitaker, 1993).

Cognitive coaching scenarios use reflection as the ideal process for training both a mentor and novice. The cognitive coaching model enables teachers to grow professionally by engaging in helpful supportive and constructive dialogues with knowledgable experts. Sparks and Hirsh (1997) contend that cognitive coaching allows teachers to have conversations with each other about professional decisions that are all developed through reflective discussions.

"Reflective teaching emphasizes the importance of teacher inquiry and counteracts a more limited interest in teachers' behavior, without considering what is going on in their minds and hearts" (Valli, 1997, p. 67). The end of a cognitive coaching session enables the coach to mediate by having teachers extend their thinking, challenge perspectives, and revise the intellectual elements involved in teaching.

The scenario in table 5.1 provides an example of using the reflective conference coupled with elements of critical thinking. This professional dialogue gives both the novice and the expert the opportunity to engage

Table 5.1. Mediation of Reflection

Reflection Scenario

My science lesson did not exactly go as planned! I thought that I had everything prepared. My materials for the experiment were on the lab stations; the students were all in groups; and the papers to record the answers were passed out. As soon as I turned around, the entire lesson fell apart. I heard a loud explosion, the room filled with screams, and then laughter. One group of students turned on the burner, heated the surface, and caused an explosion. Thankfully, no one was hurt, but the lesson was over! What went wrong?

Teacher (Novice) Responses	Cognitive Coach (Expert) Probes and Questions	Elements of Language and Thought Prompts/Questions/Comments
What went wrong with the lesson?	What are your initial thoughts about the lesson?	Point of View This question provides the expert with information from the novice as a way to initiate the novice's thinking from an individual perspective
	I see many things that did go right: your materials were prepared, your lesson was planned, your students were in groups and ready to work.	Praise and Affirmation: The expert builds confidence and trust with the teacher.

Teacher (Novice)	Cognitive Coach (Expert) Scaffolded Language	Critical Thinking Prompts/Questions/Comments
I believe that I failed at the beginning of the lesson to give clear directions to my students.	So what I hear you saying is that you think the directions should have been clearly explained prior to assigning groups?	Type of Reflection: Teacher is reflecting-on-instruction. Paraphrasing: The expert is able to restate the intent of the message by rewording and clarifying the message from the novice.
Yes, the students were eager to begin the experiment and did not listen to directions.		
Well, sometimes their behaviors are unpredictable, and some students in the groups are attention seekers.	Knowing this about some of your students, what kind of changes would you make?	Probing: This communication skill allows the expert the opportunity to gather precise and accurate information.

(continued)

Table 5.1.   (*continued*)

Teacher (Novice	Cognitive Coach (Expert)	Critical Thinking Prompts/Questions/Comments
I definitely need to have members of the groups assigned for a different reason, such as, have a leader in each group and have the attention-seeking students separated.	Great, you are really thinking this through. So you plan to assign group members, select a group leader, and separate the attention-seeking students before giving out the lab assignments or equipment. I look forward to collaborating with you on planning for the next lab. Thank you.	Praising, Paraphrasing, and Logical Clarification: The expert is able to affirm the teacher's thoughts, paraphrase to restate, and logically clarify what the novice recommended. Logical clarification allows for sensible and methodical thought to a situation that requires a combination of steps.

in thoughtful discourse, think critically, and push the boundaries of their learning.

As noted in the table, the traditional cognitive coaching model initially begins by the novice teacher evaluating whether actions were appropriate, inappropriate, effective, or ineffective. This type of self-inquiry is the beginning of reflection. According to research results (Flores, 1991), initial professional training followed by coaching resulted in a higher level of implementation than training alone.

Cognitive coaching helps teachers implement new teaching strategies, increase classroom management skills, and improve relationships with students. With cognitive coaching added to traditional staff development, the implementation level of new strategies reached 85 percent as compared to only 10 percent with the traditional delivery method. Cognitive coaching allows for precise nurturing language and critical thought; ultimately, changing teacher actions, beliefs, and cognitive abilities is the result of cognitive coaching.

Pause to Think . . .

In your teaching career, describe a time when you felt supported and coached in a professional development situation. Describe the situation, the coaching processes, thinking strategies, questioning techniques, and the results.

INSTRUCTIONAL SCAFFOLDING

The primary aspect of cognitive coaching is the social interaction and use of language, either conversations or dialogues between the professionals. One dimension of structured language is the use of scaffolding. Instructional scaffolding refers to the process that enables a novice and an expert to solve a problem or achieve a goal beyond the realm of unassisted efforts (Wood, Bruner, & Ross, 1976). For example, when teaching someone to play a new game, the instructions are given step-by-step by the expert. Next, there is an opportunity to play only the beginning portion of the game, followed by supportive correction by the expert, if needed. Additional instructions for the game are given, with opportunities to play without assistance. Ultimately, the novice is able to play the game alone with initial support and encouragement from the expert.

Interaction between professionals in a cognitive coaching venue uses scaffolded language to influence decision making, thought, and ultimately professional practice with the novice. Scaffolding is used to describe the tutorial assistance provided by the expert who is in control of those elements that are beyond the capabilities of the novice (Wood, Bruner, & Ross, 1976). These scaffolds are intended to be temporary, fluid, and adjustable, with the novice ultimately able to take on the task or skill independently.

Pause to Think . . .

Think of a time when someone helped you think through a new task using the process of scaffolding. What new task or skill were you trying to learn? Describe the experience. How did you learn the new skill or task? Was the learning experience worthwhile? How can you apply this skill to your classroom?

Central to instructional scaffolding is Vygotsky's (1978) zone of proximal development, as defined by "the distance between the actual development level as determined by independent problem-solving and the level of potential development as determined through problem-solving under adult guidance, or in collaboration with more capable peers" (p. 86). Vygotsky's attempt to explain the relationship between learning and mental development is fully described in the collaborative interaction between a novice and an expert. "Scaffolding can be a powerful analytic tool in examining what teachers do to help students learn to read and write" (p. 169).

Scaffolded instruction provides a temporary support system for the novice (Cazden, 1983), which encourages increased learning and cognitive growth. Individuals are able to interact with peers at optimum levels of cognitive operations, which result in increased thinking, improved decision making, and professional judgments that can be generalized across a variety of situations.

The supportive guidance from an expert enables individuals to eventually develop new skills independently. Social interactions between the novice and expert support the development of higher-order mental processes. These higher-order cognitive processes occur first in the social plane, with others, and later alone on the individual plane. As the novice and the expert work together, it is possible to reach higher levels of cognitive awareness through dialogue, conversation, and discussion that is impossible for the novice to reach independently.

SOCIAL INTERACTION

Functioning in a supportive, communicative setting involving the interactions with others allows for self-regulation to develop (Wertsch, 1979). Self-regulation of tasks is a gradual process and is a result of the novice assuming responsibilities from the expert. Eventually, as the novice feels confident with the task, is able to initiate the actions of the expert, and can independently perform the task, the novice is independent; for example, a child is learning to ride a bicycle with the support of training wheels. Eventually, the training wheels are ready to be removed, and the child must begin to take on more of the tasks of balancing and riding the bike.

As the training wheels are removed, a supportive caregiver assists and guides as the child learns to balance and ride alone. The caregiver runs behind the child with a hand on the back seat and slowly removes the support as the child becomes stable. As the child masters the new task of riding a bike, there are a few unsteady times with the child weaving back and forth, but the caregiver is close by, ready to give support and encouragement. Ultimately, the child is independent and ready to ride the bike alone.

The child is considered able to self-regulate the process of bike riding. The child is able to get up after a fall and ride again immediately, with minor adjustments. The child may be wobbly at first, adjusting from side to side, but soon the child will be able to adjust and ride confidently. Moving to self-regulated is many times not a fluid or immediate process. With practice and supportive interaction, novices are able to move to self-regulation with most new tasks in a relatively short time frame.

Researchers investigated dialogue in a variety of settings for supporting the acquisition of knowledge and the continual improvement in instructional methods (Applebee & Langer, 1983; Wood, Bruner, & Ross, 1976). The role of scaffolded dialogue in instruction has been studied in the areas of reading and writing (Applebee & Langer, 1983), comprehension (Pearson & Gallagher, 1983), and reciprocal teaching (Brown & Palinscar, 1985). The extensive research conducted in a variety of curricular areas support the attainment of new knowledge in a supportive environment as a way to increase professional performance and student achievement.

Pause to Think . . .

Think of a task that you have been able to achieve through the support of others. At what point in the learning process did you feel self-regulated? What were your clues that you were independent with the new task?

Dewey (1933) recognized that individuals *reflect* on a whole host of things in the sense of merely *thinking about* them; however, logical or *analytic* reflection can happen only when there is a real problem to solve. Dewey saw true reflective practice as taking place when the individual faces a real problem that needs to be resolved in a rational manner. He attested that reflection begins with a *felt difficulty* that can range in intensity from mild uneasiness to intense shock. To address this range of emotion, Dewey suggested that individuals proceed through three steps of reflection:

- problem identification
- analysis
- generalization

BLOGS AND JOURNALS TO SUPPORT REFLECTION

To become effectively student-centered, professionals must maintain a continual level of constructive self-questioning, develop the ability to view situations from many perspectives, and use the results of reflective thought.

In a study conducted by Bruster, Peterson, and Pirkle (2009), eighteen teacher candidates kept weekly reflections on individual clinical teaching placements. These reflections were recorded in diary-style journals and teacher online blogs. There were nine participants who used the traditional journaling technique and nine who reflected using online blogs.

The participants in the blog group wrote affirming comments and suggestions to one another and wrote more frequently. The journaling group wrote one reflective essay weekly, sharing the reflection only with the university supervisor. After evaluating the groups, there were differences between the two groups. For example, those writing in the formal diary-style journal appeared to write complex investigative types of reflections, expressing in their writing a depth of understanding of theory applied to practice. Those who wrote blogs appeared to write less complex descriptions of classroom events. Some expressed questions about the meaning of the events, about solving problems and analyzing the problems, and about connecting theory correctly.

While these are important findings, those who wrote in the blog also participated in electronic conversations with one another and established a supportive *professional learning community*. The degree of trust, comfort, and support was evident in their reflections.

The writing style of the blogging group appeared relaxed and informal. A free-flowing of ideas exchanged among participants in the blogging group indicated the emergence of a professional learning community. Participants were able to voice concerns about specific situations and immediately had supportive responses from peers or professors who also were contributing to the blog. Additionally, teacher candidates were able to confirm beliefs and validate feelings.

Additional findings from this study included the analysis of language found in the reflection blogs verses the language found in the journals. There were 132 total reflective entries analyzed to determine specific language attributes between the two groups. After analyzing and comparing the blog reflections to the journal reflections, the following differences were noted. The language used in the journaling group was formal and structured, whereas the blogging group was more informal and conversational, as shown by the following:

- Some 24 percent of the blogs were supportive in nature.
- Diary-style journaling reflective entries did not use supportive language.
- Affirmative or supportive language was found in fifteen of forty-three blog reflections.
- Five instances of requests for advice with a particular situation were found in the blogging reflections.

The teacher candidates in the blogging group were extremely comfortable communicating with each other and exhibited a close working relationship in a trusting online environment. By connecting the essential elements of cognitive coaching to the reflective process, teacher candidates were able to develop greater precise language in the blogs, facilitate thinking, and build professional confidence. In the blogging scenarios, teacher candidates developed autonomy, efficacy, and self-awareness. The findings of this single study provided insight into reflection and the impact of cognitive coaching on teacher dialogue.

Pause to Think . . .

Have you had the opportunity to use a teacher blog, online network, or reflection journal as a way to interact with other professionals? If so, were you able to solve some of your instructional or classroom challenges? Did you feel at ease discussing instructional issues? Did you find it helpful?

Using reflective blogs coupled with components of cognitive coaching has tremendous potential for increased professional growth. Essential components of traditional coaching must be present for coaching to occur effectively in the online blogs. The blogging atmosphere must be safe, free from threat, and supportive in nature.

The *bloggers* must feel that sound professional relationships are present before true interactions can begin. Online venues allow for professional development opportunities in a safe and threat-free environment. Blogging provides an opportunity for professional collegiality and establishes an opportunity to collectively problem solve.

CHAPTER SUMMARY

The use of dialogue, conversation, and cognitive coaching skills are essential communication tools for effective teaching. This chapter focused on the critical nature of these communication skills coupled with precise language as a way to enhance reflection. The social process of reflection and elements of cognitive coaching are combined to scaffold professional reflection. The use of dialogue and cognitive coaching are both excellent venues for improving reflection. The social negotiation of meaning using precise nurturing language is enhanced by analyzing dialogue within the context of blogging and reflective-style journaling to influence professional decisions and the reflective process.

CHAPTER STUDY QUESTIONS

After reading this chapter, use these questions to discuss with your colleagues:

1. How important is dialogue in the reflective process?
2. What are the critical aspects of cognitive coaching, and how can these improve reflections?
3. Define scaffolding and provide an example.
4. List the three steps that individuals proceed through to reflection, and give an example.
5. What are the critical components of blogging as it relates to cognitive coaching?

PROBLEM SETS/ACTIVITIES

In teams of two, take on a role, an expert cognitive coach or an inexperienced novice teacher. Use varied cognitive coaching prompts or critical-thinking questions to provide support for the novice teacher. As an expert cognitive coach, provide assistance for this novice teacher; use varied cognitive coaching prompts or critical-thinking questions to provide support and guidance through these scenarios. Use table 5.1 for support, if needed.

1. This year is my first year teaching in a fourth-grade classroom. I believe I work very hard and am adequately prepared. I plan extensively, and I know my lesson objectives. I believe in teaching with a hands-on lesson approach. One particular lesson was on measurement, and I made sure that my students understood the concept of measuring weight before the class began. The objective of the lesson was to reinforce the concept of using the scientific method of investigation and recording results. I began the lesson by placing my students in groups of four in anticipation that students would quickly know what to do once they were in the assigned group. I quickly realized that my students did not seem to have a clue how to begin. My students all began asking questions and were completely confused with where to begin or what to do first.
2. I am an eighth-grade English teacher. I think that I have good relationships with most of my students, but I am having extreme difficulty with one particular student, Joe. Joe is extremely argumentative and defiant. I have tried a few things that I thought would help but, so far, his behavior is not any better. I had an idea that I could improve my relationship

with Joe by establishing a relationship with his mother. I thought that I may be having difficulty with Joe because he has a very poor attitude and appears to have no friends in class. I decided to contact his parents; however, I am a new teacher and I have limited experience with contacting parents. I am at a loss about approaching these parents. They did not attend *Meet the Teacher Night* held earlier in the year and have not responded to any e-mails. Joe is very bright, possibly gifted, but he also likes to argue with me and deliberately puts me into unproductive discussions. This behavior then affects other students in the classroom, and more students are beginning to be argumentative. I need some ideas and help with this situation.

BIBLIOGRAPHY

Applebee, A. N., & Langer, J. (1983). Instructional scaffolding: Reading and writing are natural language activities. *Language Arts, 60*(2), 168–175.

Brown, A. L., & Palinscar, A. S. (1985). Reciprocal teaching of comprehension strategies: A natural history of one program for enhancing learning. (Technical Report No. 334.) Champaign, IL: University of Illinois.

Bruner, J. S. (1966). *Toward a theory of instruction.* New York: W. W. Norton & Co., Inc.

Bruster, B., Peterson, B., & Pirkle, S. (2009). *Transforming reflective practice: Using blogs and journaling with teacher candidates.* Unpublished manuscript submitted for publication.

Cazden, C. B. (1983). Adult assistance in language development: Scaffolds, models, and direct instruction. In R. P. Parker & F. A. Davis (Eds.), *Developing literacy: Young children's use of language* (pp. 3–18). Newark, DE: International Reading Association.

Costa, A. L., & Garmston, R. J. (1994). *Cognitive coaching: A foundation for renaissance schools.* Norwood, MA: Christopher-Gordon Publishers.

Costa, A. L., & Kallick, B. (2008). *Learning and leading with habits of mind: 16 essential characteristics for success.* Norwood, MA: Christopher-Gordon Publishers.

Dewey, J. (1933). *How we think.* Chicago: Henry Regnery.

Edwards, P. A. (1995). Empowering low-income mothers and fathers to share books with young children. *The Reading Teacher, 48,* 558–565.

Flores, J. (1991). *Cognitive coaching: Does it help?* Master's Thesis, Educational Administration, California State University, Sacramento, CA.

Garmston, R. J., Linder, C., & Whitaker, J. (1993). Reflections on cognitive coaching. *Educational Leadership, 51*(2), 57–61.

Pearson, P. D., & Gallagher, M.C. (1983). The instruction of reading comprehension. *Contemporary Educational Psychology, 8,* 317–344.

Showers, B., & Joyce, B. (1996). The evolution of peer coaching. *Educational Leadership, 53*(6), 12–16.

Sparks, D., & Hirsh, S. (1997). *A new vision for staff development.* Alexandria, VA: ASCD.

Valli, L. (1997). Listening to other voices: A description of teacher reflection in the United States. *Peabody Journal of Education, 72*(1), 67–88.

Vygotsky, L. S. (1978). *Mind in society.* Cambridge, MA: Harvard University Press.

Vygotsky, L. S. (1986). *Thought and language.* Cambridge, MA: MIT Press.

Wertsch, J. V. (1979). From social interaction to higher psychological processes: A clarification and application of Vygotsky's theory. *Human Development, 22,* 1–22.

Wood, D., Bruner, J. S., & Ross, G. (1976). The role of tutoring in problem solving. *Child Psychologists, 17,* 89–100.

Chapter Six

Critical Thinking Enhancing Phases of Reflection

Any experience, however trivial in its first appearance, is capable of assuming an indefinite richness of significance by extending its range of
perceived connection (Dewey, 1916, p. 225).

OVERVIEW

In this chapter, the importance of reflective practice and the use of reflection
to influence professional decision making is outlined. Different phases of
reflection are identified, and each phase is categorized and described using
language that assists in the identification of reflective thought. During reflection, there are clearly different levels of language, thought, and reflective
practice among individuals.

Research results indicated (Schön, 1983; Valli, 1992; Zeichner & Liston,
1996) that professionals reflect at different levels, use different types of
reflection, and reflect for different purposes. In this chapter, it is presented
that explicit language clearly identifies phases of reflection and descrip-
tors that relate to each specific phase. Each phase actively demonstrates
the use of universal critical-thinking standards that directly align to each
phase of reflection. By understanding the phases of reflection and the impact of integrating critical thinking, professionals can improve their future
practice and ultimately become cognizant of reflective thought as a routine
practice.

REFLECTIVE THINKING AND
PROFESSIONAL DEVELOPMENT

Dewey (1933) indicated that reflective thought is necessary because it releases individuals from merely impulsive and routine activity. Reflection engages individual intelligent thought and action resulting in informed decisions.

Reflective thought enables individuals to:

• direct activities with foresight.
• plan according to an end-in-view.
• develop an awareness of thinking.

Learning is an active process that results in change (Piaget, 1967). New information must assimilate or accommodate with other learning experiences before it can be meaningful or useful. Assimilation allows new information to be reconstructed in ways that integrate the information into existing background knowledge. In order to assimilate information, reflective thought is critical to the process. The degree to which the information is assimilated depends in great part on reflection and on the critical events that surround the new information.

Consider the following example of a hypotherical critical event, in which the parental involvement at Caldwell Elementary School was minimal. Upon gathering information and reflecting on possible causes of limited parental involvement, the following issues were discovered:

• students at the school were highly mobile.
• three hundred of the families at Caldwell were Spanish speaking.
• formal parent groups at Caldwell were not accommodating to new families.
• parent materials and communications were only in English.

The limited parental involvement, coupled with critical analysis and reflective thought, resulted in the assimilation of new information before decisions were reached and problems were resolved. Prior knowledge of English language learners (ELL), a cultural understanding of families at the school, and community awareness were all important factors that resulted in effective actions.

Accommodation allows for the reconstruction of new information by making changes to existing background knowledge, thereby changing thought and creating new knowledge. Reflection is one way to effectively assimilate and accommodate new learning.

Dewey explained, "Education consists of the formation of wide-awake, careful, thorough habits of thinking" (1933, p. 78). Dewey (1964) also noted that traditional teacher-training programs failed to connect the technical competencies that are required of teachers to the thought processes of their students. For example, a math teacher may have the technical understanding of teaching students addition facts but may fail to connect a technical knowledge base and methods of teaching to the developmental needs of students. Developmentally, students need math manipulatives for accurately solving addition problems, but the teacher provides only math worksheets for students to complete.

Novice teachers with traditional training merely modeled or imitated classroom behaviors but failed to connect philosophies that informed their decisions. This type of mindless teaching only leads to unreflective thought, rote behaviors, and limited repertoires of practice. Teachers who fail to reflect will ultimately become unresponsive, experience burnout, and leave the profession. Unreflective teaching may ultimately result in unresponsive teaching and low-achieving students. Students become complacent with the *sit and get* routines of teachers who continue to do things the same way, day after day, year after year.

Schön (1987) described teaching as an unpredictable and uncertain process. Teaching is multifaceted, and the application of new information simply cannot be forced into routine, stagnant environments where change is not embraced. Teaching is a dynamic and constantly changing profession. Reflective thought applied to the teaching process is like trying to repair a jet plane in midflight. The flight must continue, there is a planned destination, the passengers are all present; however, the flight plan is set and the plane cannot stop or change its course. As a teacher, the students are all present, the teaching is underway, but learning is not occurring. The lesson plan is set and instruction must continue. The scope and sequence of the curriculum is an expectation, and state standardized assessments are looming. There is little time to reflect on the act of teaching, and resources are limited. Just as in the jet plane metaphor, the plane must be repaired in midflight or a crash is inevitable. The instructional methods used and the teacher's knowledge must be refined or the students will ultimately fail!

Staying the course is not the best option. Explicit instructional tools and reflective examination are needed to make desired changes. Experienced and effective reflective practitioners are able to make these *in-flight* changes with ease and grace.

Using reflection to change practice is paramount to quality teaching. Positive changes can occur that result in professional growth by effectively using the reflective process at pivotal points along the way. Teachers must

use critical-thinking skills effectively in decision making to fully understand the power of reflection and to experience the impacts on instructional
practice.

Pause to Think . . .

Think of a time in your life that an event or an experience changed or
redirected your future. What part did reflective thought play in the change
process?

PHASES OF REFLECTION

The purpose of the following section is to assist individuals with identifying
reflective thought, to clarify individual phases of reflection, and to provide
examples of these different phases. An in-depth investigation of reflective
phases, using examples of critical thinking questions and prompts, provides
clarification for each phase. The active reflective process requires movement
in and out of the different phases as well as an understanding of critical thinking as it applies to reflection and professional change.

Five Phases of Reflection

1. Descriptive Phase—Professionals at the descriptive phase of reflection often limit their perceptions to isolated events. Events are simply described
   with limited elaborations or interactions with others. Many times events
   are reported with little or no consideration or connection to the individual
   lives or professions. Individuals at this phase describe events as looking
   down on a situation, simply reporting with limited personal or professional
   investment. The description may involve a situation, an event, a project, or
   possibly actions taken related to this event.

   Included in this description may be the setting and observations of a
   situation. Individuals comply with the requirements to reflect with virtually no critical thought applied to the process. Individuals at this phase
   have limited experiences and are typically novices and beginning practitioners. Professional growth is seldom impacted by this narrow reflection,
   causing accommodation or assimilation of information extremely difficult.
   Individuals at this phase have a narrowed perspective and a limited professional bank of experiences.

Pause to Think . . .

Reflections at the Descriptive Phase:

1. After reading this scenario, what attributes qualify as the descriptive phase of reflection?

I taught Language Arts today. I was worried about the fact that another teacher warned me several times that the class was a handful, but I felt that my experience went quite well. The students identified prepositional phrases, adverbs, adjectives, and pronouns in the paragraph, and I briefly discussed each. The class then split into groups where I worked with one group on the parts of speech. The remainder of the students worked on posters that they were to share with the class.

2. Think of your own examples of a reflection at the descriptive phase.

2. Inquisitive Phase—Individuals at this phase of reflection begin to question practice and examine professional choices by formulating inquiries about actions. Initial thoughts and questions at this phase are based on limited experiences as well as incomplete knowledge bases. Individuals apply their limited professional knowledge at a surface level only with minimal understandings. In addition, they question their ability to adequately complete a job, handle a crisis, or understand a critical incident.

Individuals realize that problems exist but have a limited repertoire of skills and knowledge. Professional choices are questioned, but individuals at the inquisitive phase do not have ample experiences with reoccurring situations or opportunities to apply changes.

For example, an unpleasant or upsetting event or situation occurred, but individuals are unable to take actions. At the inquisitive phase, individuals simply recognize the incident but hope that it will never happen again. After reflection, the problem or critical incident was identified; however, failure to act or move further than self-questioning is the extent of the reflection. This inquisitive phase includes all the elements of the descriptive level, and individuals will not move beyond the attributes of this level when reflecting.

Pause to Think . . .

Reflections at the Inquisitive Phase:

1. After reading the following scenarios, what attributes qualify as the inquisitive phase of reflection?

Scenario # 1

I want to try a new activity, but I am not sure how the students will react. I need to find an easier way to present the material. Again, I am still not quite sure of what is *over the heads* of my students and what is not. Last year, I taught fourth grade. First-graders are so different!

Scenario # 2

My teaching experience on Friday while teaching reading: there were two literacy centers and the students rotated between the centers every thirty minutes. My lesson was not a *crash and burn*. . . . that was good, but I might be too critical of myself. I felt like I did an awful job, and some of my students did not care about the planned lesson one way or the other. I was not sure what to do or what to try!

2. Think of times in your career where you felt this way about your decisions, thought processes, or lessons.

3. What type of decisions did you make? What were the results?

3. Investigative Phase—Individuals at this reflective phase are able to identify critical incidents, and they begin to investigate solutions for problems. They examine alternative practices and choices based on prior experiences, opinions of others, or new information. They search for information to specific questions, concerns, or problems using a variety of methods, continually researching new techniques until possible resolutions are found.

Individuals begin to investigate theories and applications based on their knowledge or the knowledge of others. They try to find their professional identity, use professional intuition, and, at times, connect decisions with past experiences, theories, or content information. These individuals are constantly searching for clarification, verification, and validation of their emerging habits, knowledge, and personal theories. Professionals at this level can make decisions spontaneously, *on-the-run*, with confidence based on their knowledge base and effective connections to past experiences.

Pause to Think . . .

Reflections at the Investigative Phase:

1. After reading the following scenarios, what attributes qualify them as the investigative phase of reflection?

Scenario # 1

Friday was a wonderful learning experience for me. I was a part of the grade-level group. I must say that I am working with a wonderful group of teachers! We were able to help each other in so many ways. Our lead teacher is also excellent and provided me with excellent feedback to my questions.

Scenario # 2

One thing that needs definite improvement is the pacing of my lesson. There are times when I was so concerned about not filling the time allotted for the lesson that I let the discussion drag on and on because I was unsure of what to do next.

2. Describe a professional situation or incident that happened.

3. What are some options and alternatives that align with the characteristics of the investigative phase?

4. Interdependent Phase—Individuals at this reflective phase are able to combine an understanding of theory with practice. They are able to consider academic programs, resources, and options when planning for the well-being of others. Intellectual growth is only one component for the fulfillment of student needs. Other considerations are the social, emotional, and physical needs essential for development and improvement. They are effective problem-solvers who consider the dispositional, contextual, and environmental factors of learning, growth, and change.

The cultural diversity, economic factors, and individual characteristics of everyone involved are considered in the decision-making process. Professional goals are set based on identified needs or situational conditions. For example, students in a high-need school with low academic achievement have multiple factors that impact their achievement. Teachers in schools with compounding factors effecting achievement must be able to effectively reflect by connecting professional philosophies, theories, and current research. Teachers at the interdependent phase have in-depth content knowledge and are able to effectively problem-solve with assurance and sustainability.

Reflections at the Interdependent Phase:

1. After reading these scenarios, what attributes qualify them as the interdependent phase of reflection?

Scenario # 1

I believe that I have an exceptional class this year; however, one of my students always appears to be withdrawn and never plays with others. I know that English is not her first language. Perhaps I need to meet with her parents and get some additional information about her family. I can arrange some *community building activities* in my classroom as a way to get everyone acquainted and involved.

Scenario # 2

Several students in my classroom do not know their multiplication facts very well. Some of the other students make fun of them, but I stop that immediately because I know how hurtful that is. We have a new computer math program at school. I will give my students needing help with math additional time and extra practice on the computer. I think this will help them with the multiplication skill gaps. Next, I must find some type of program for bullying and teasing behaviors. I think this may be occurring in my classroom.

2. Think of situations in your classroom when your reflections were at the interdependent phase.

3. What were your reactions or solutions to these learning opportunities?

5. Global Phase—Individuals at this phase begin to address moral and ethical issues as well as the multiple factors affecting the situation. They practice self-discipline and self-understanding by considering ethical, moral, and political issues around them. Problem solving takes on another dimension as cultural, ethical, and social aspects of the environment, the community, and the world are considered. Individual reflections at this phase consider issues in relation to the future of the profession as well as how factors are interrelated in the world.

   Social action and political influences to policies result from global reflections. At this phase, professionals are confident in their content knowledge and continually seek information for global improvement. Van Manen (1977) referred to this level of reflection as critical reflection. Individuals at this level deal with moral and ethical issues that directly relate to their professional practice. For example, individuals in this phase of reflection make decisions for the best interest of everyone involved. Based on knowledge, experiences, and research, professionals at the global phase recognize the interconnectedness of all decisions and act accordingly.

Pause to Think . . .

Reflections at the Global Phase:

1. After reading these scenarios, what attributes qualify them as the inter-dependent phase of reflection?

Scenario # 1

I currently teach high school English, and, for months, I have tried every trick in my bag to get one of my students to read. He simply will not read any of his assignments, and he does not read for pleasure. One day last week, he brought a book to class and, during silent reading time, I found him reading the entire time. After class, I asked him about the book he had chosen, and when he told me about it, I found myself perplexed. The book was about the Mafia and filled with killing and real-life situations. There were even guides telling how to become a Mafia member. Ethically, this is not the type of book that I want my high school students reading. I am trying to think about how I should handle this delicate situation.

Scenario # 2

I have had some interesting results this year with my middle school science labs. I currently teach eighth-grade science, and I have been experimenting with setting up the weekly science labs using the varied learning styles of my students. Each student can select the activity that suites his/her learning style preference and then complete that particular lab. My results have been outstanding. These lab techniques are very helpful to my students, and I believe other teachers will benefit from the information. I am planning to write a training manual to share with other middle school science teachers and then present this information at the National Middle School Conference in the spring.

2. What are your experiences with reflection at the global phase?

As practitioners assign labels to reflection, the identification of specific language patterns and characteristics emerge at each phase and provide insight for reflection. Preliminary research indicates that the most occurring phase of reflection can be identified as the descriptive or inquisitive phase. Richardson (1990) noted that individuals do not naturally think in a descriptive mode, but this mode most commonly occurs first.

New information may be taught to others only if adequate time is provided and background experiences relate to new information in meaningful ways. Opportunities for working with others, time to feel comfortable in the learning environment, and respect from peers and teachers are critical before individuals are able to move effortlessly within the phases.

Pause to Think . . .

1. When you learn new teaching techniques or have new programs to incorporate into your curriculum, how do you assimilate and/or accommodate this information in ways that are meaningful to you?

2. Think of examples.

3. What are useful techniques, and how are these incorporated into your teaching experiences? (If needed, use the information in this chapter on assimilation and accommodation.)

Reflective practice is a vital key for professional growth by incorporating new information, skills, and techniques into individuals' professional repertoire. Being cognizant of the varied phases of reflection is only the first step in using reflection to change professional practice. Working in a climate that is reflective, vibrant, and promotes the development of collaborative skills is essential to productive reflective thought. The research and information on critical-thinking habits are examined as an important component for improving and changing reflective practice.

COGNITION: A SOCIAL PROCESS

The development of cognitive control and critical thinking is a social process. Connections between the quality of reflections coupled with critical self-questioning and prompts influence professional decisions. Individuals experience problem solving in the presence of others and gradually begin to perform the task alone. Consider the following example: an individual is trying to learn a new electronic game on the computer. The game is purchased, all the directions are read, and the game is played several times. However, it is discovered that there are parts to the game that are found by talking with other game players who have experienced the game. Finding someone else who is an *expert* in the game is probably one of the fastest and most efficient ways to improve. To begin the learning process, the player must have conversations with others in the virtual game world and find shortcuts and secrets to the game that are impossible to find alone.

Pause to Think . . .

Think of a time when you experienced problem-solving with the help of another teacher or mentor.

Describe the experiences you had.

In order for individuals to increase their learning, a variety of instructional settings, experiences, and challenges must be present to enhance learning opportunities. Taking on new tasks and making those tasks personal require practice and working closely with others who are invested in the new learning. Making a new skill permanent is a gradual process.

The acquisition of new information requires the continual practice and rehearsal of all skills before making them a permanent way of thinking or responding. As new behaviors and tasks are acquired, the new skills associated with the tasks need extensive practice in varied environments, coupled with continued support from others invested in the learning. Gradually, over time, new tasks become comfortable and routine, and professionals are able to move through the skills required in the new tasks with ease (Wertsch, 1979). Practicing and rehearsing the steps in a task until the tasks are repeatable and routine is the key to stabilizing new learning.

For individuals to become reflective problem-solvers, the environment must be stable and supportive in nature. Independent thinkers and problem-solvers are connected and engaged in supportive reflection with a mentor or lead teacher. Teachers improve their thinking and knowledge by interactions and intellectual challenges and models such as thinking aloud.

Thinking aloud is a process where individual thoughts are verbalized, and professionals are able to model and clarify thought processes and actions. Using the think-aloud process with other professionals to share reflections improves professional understandings. Individuals use their thought processes as a model and are able to verbalize their thoughts (Davey, 1983).

As individuals are trained to use cognitive processes such as think-alouds, cognitive coaching, and critical-thinking questions, complex thought can generate and fuel the process of in-depth reflective thinking. According to Elder and Paul (2008), there are stages of critical-thinking development. The stages of critical thinking are as follows:

- unreflective—unaware of significant problems in our thinking
- challenged—faced with problems in thinking

- beginning—trying to improve without systematic regular thinking
- practicing—recognizing the need for regular practice
- advanced—keeping with practice
- master—good habits of thought that are becoming second nature

CRITICAL THINKING

Critical thinking is the ability to analyze, evaluate, and interpret thoughts, free from bias and prejudice. Critical thinking is dynamic and continually changing. For example, all thinking is dependent upon our experiences, the learning environments, and one's subjective thoughts, feelings, and beliefs. Critical thinking in the reflection process is the ability to self-monitor personal events and the ability to use information in ways that affect current or future actions (Argyris, 1992; Brookfield, 1995; Tennyson, 1990; 1992).

By effectively weaving critical thinking into personal reflection, changes to professional practice can occur. "Everyone thinks, it is our nature to do so. But much of our thinking, left to itself, is biased, distorted, partial, uninformed, or down-right prejudiced" (Elder & Paul, 2008, p. 2). As thought processes are actively identified and practiced, it is possible to influence reflective thinking to span the phases from the descriptive to global.

By teaching the elements of critical thinking applied to reflection, effective habits typically are nurtured and continually practiced in a variety of settings before inefficient habits begin to form. According to Elder and Paul, "Critical thinking is the art of analyzing and evaluating thinking with a view to improve it" (2008, p. 2). A well-cultivated thinker has the following abilities:

- formulate questions that are clear and precise.
- engage in dialogue with knowledgable others.
- consider the process of thinking: planned, systematic, and proactive.
- attention to and an organization of content.
- connecting assumptions to reasoning.
- creating intellectual constructs or "hooks" as a way to connect new information.

Tennyson (1990; 1992) concluded that contextual learning is a progression from *knowing that* to *knowing how* to *knowing why*. Critical thinking is putting into practice, making connections, and differentiating between *the how* and *the why* of what is done in the classroom. Ultimately being able to integrate and construct new habits of thinking will allow reflective thought to evolve into a deeper and more meaningful process. Critical thinking allows for self-monitoring and provides for effective problem solving across a variety of situations.

In the following section, the use of critical-thinking questions and probes during reflection are used to influence and ultimately change the actions of professionals. According to Elder and Paul (2008), there are universal intellectual standards for critical thinking and questions that can be used as a way to apply these standards. The Universal Standards of Critical Thinking are as follows:

1. clarity—we need a clear and consistent understanding of the content.
2. accuracy—we must determine if the statement is factual and true.
3. precision—the information must be specific in nature.
4. relevance—the content included must be connected.
5. depth—the significant issues and information are included.
6. breadth—all points of view must be considered.
7. logic—we must have relevant reasoning.
8. significance—we must consider all important information.
9. fairness—we must consider all relevant points of view.

Using universal thinking standards to effectively probe and question individuals during reflection is essential to learning to think critically. It also improves the quality of thinking about professional practice. Reflections are influenced by explicitly teaching the universal standards and infusing the language into professional dialogue with others. Examples of critical-thinking standards and precise language are applied to reflection scenarios as a way to enhance professional decision making and, ultimately, influence professional practice. Table 6.1 contains examples of probes and questions that represent ways to enhance reflective thought.

After applying the Universal Standards of Critical Thinking to reflection, there are many extended opportunities for professionals to engage in self-questioning. The primary purpose of these questions and prompts is to engage professionals in analytical thinking. Teachers delve deeply into their own thinking and the thinking of others, which results in higher levels of thinking and improved professional practice.

When considering the phases of reflection, the use of questions and probes can encourage dialogue between professionals and has the potential to change present or future actions. As individuals begin to use reflective phases to identify thought, it is important to remember that the reflective process is fluid and that individuals move in and out of each phase depending on situations. Reaching a deeper understanding of an issue is possible by using the critical-thinking questions at any phase. With extensive practice, quality thinking

Table 6.1. Reflection Scenarios

Read these scenarios in this table. Use the critical-thinking probes and questions in the center column as models to influence the scenarios and responses.

Reflection Scenarios	Critical-Thinking Universal Standards	Reflection Reflection Scenarios
Reflection: Descriptive Phase My activity to help my students with word fluency was a bingo game and a partner exercise. The bingo game words came from the shared reading book. Five of the words were their vocabulary words. After a few games of bingo, I will pair up the students and they will have the list of vocabulary words on a rubric. My students will enjoy the bingo game.	Clarity: Probes and Questions 1. Give some examples of how the students responded. 2. Tell me more about the success of the students.	Reflection: Inquisitive Phase This activity helped my students practice for the word fluency and parts of the upcoming Dibels test. All but five of my twenty-three students were successful. Please leave comments on how you feel about my activity. I would appreciate any feedback!
Reflection: Descriptive Phase My lesson was much too long. The clock was running so fast that there was so much of my lesson left incomplete. Time management needs work again. My lesson was much longer than I expected.	Accuracy: Probes and Questions 1. Exactly how much time was over at the end of the activity? 2. How much content could you have omitted and still been within the given time frame?	Reflection: Investigative Phase My lesson was much longer than I expected. As I think back over my lesson, there are several items that I can omit and rearrange in order to save time. I am excited to teach this lesson again and try some of my time-saving ideas.
Reflection: Investigative Phase Making this lesson plan wasn't the hardest thing for me to do. Making the assessments was definitely one of the hardest. It was hard for me	Precision: Probes and Questions 1. Can you be more exact in the requirements	Reflection: Interdependent Phase As I plan the assessment, I need to keep in mind the individual needs of my students and plan assessments accordingly. (continued)

Reflection Scenarios	Critical-Thinking Universal Standards	Reflection Reflection Scenarios
to stay in the mind-set that these are first graders and the whole lesson was on blending letters together to form one-syllable words. I could not for the life of me figure out how I was supposed to have them take a paper/pencil test when I thought it should be more verbal.	to be measured? 2. What type of assessment (oral, written, and so on) did you want to use?	I have several special needs students; therefore, my assessments must not only measure the standard but also be suited to meet student needs.
Reflection: Investigative Phase Many of us reflect each day probably in an informal way, such as going over those things that went wrong in our lessons or maybe an incident with a student. I believe that some formal reflection is necessary for change. I would caution, too, that we work to reflect on those things that are positive as well as those things that are negative. Remember, we should keep those strategies that work so we can realize what the positives are in our classrooms as well as the negatives.	Relevance: Probes and Questions 1. Tell me more about how reflecting on positive events can help. 2. Your example is on target, and how can we use this reflective statement to give specific examples in the future?	Reflection: Interdependent Phase Remember, we should keep those strategies that work, so we need to realize what the positives are in our classrooms as well as the negatives. We tend to reflect on the negative or the things that do not go the way we planned, such as going to the parent conference without being fully prepared. Many times, we learn what to do by making critical mistakes. Always check with a mentor or supervisor prior to your conferences to ensure that you are prepared.
Reflection: Descriptive Phase My class was out of control at the end of the period. I waited on pins and needles for the final bell to ring.	Depth: Probes and Questions 1. What kind of behaviors were you seeing that were out of control? 2. What type of behavior would you like to see?	Reflection: Investigative Phase I recently read an article about a new classroom management technique that works well for middle school students. I will try some new techniques in order to improve the behavior of my students. *(continued)*

Table 6.1. (*continued*)

Reflection Scenarios	Critical-Thinking Universal Standards	Reflection Reflection Scenarios
Reflection Investigative Phase After twenty years, I am still trying new ideas, new techniques, going to as many conferences as I can afford. I don't ever want to be boring in the classroom. Reflection is a part of my day, and it is easier now than when I first started.	Breadth: Probes and Questions 1. What are some other ways that you can keep your professional skills fine-tuned, other than conferences? 2. Can you give some rationale as to why reflection is easier after practice?	Reflection: Interdependent Phase My most recent training was on Ruby Payne's book on poverty. I am able to see many of the aspects of generational poverty in the lives of my students. This insight helps in my understanding of these students as well as helps in planning their instruction.
Reflection: Investigative Phase I constantly reflect on my teaching. I'm sure many of you can relate to this, but sometimes I even wake up in the middle of the night thinking about ideas for class or for a particular student. I think about what my classes are going to struggle with as I'm preparing for a lesson. I use observation while the lesson is happening, and after the lesson, I think of highs and lows my students achieved during the lesson and what we need to do to progress to the next lesson. I have learned so many things about incorporating vocabulary and useful literacy tools. I teach special education, and the highest	Fairness: Probes and Questions 1. Are my viewpoints and opinions represented in an open, honest, and unbiased way? 2. Am I accepting all points of view with an open mind? 3. Is this fair and equitable to all concerned?	Reflection: Global Phase I am very excited about the progress of my students; however, I really wonder if this literacy approach has excited my students and spurred their love for reading this year. I want to share this literacy approach with other teachers at the state Special Education Conference as a way to improve the reading skills of below-level and unmotivated high school readers. After this positive experience with my students, I am planning to investigate the labeling of special education students as learning disabled readers at such an early age when in reality the real problem may be motivation.

(*continued*)

Reflection Scenarios	Critical-Thinking Universal Standards	Reflection Reflection Scenarios
readers I have are on the third-grade reading level. Before this year, I would have never thought of using literacy circles with my population of students, but my kids loved it! We all worked on one book at a time since my students do not do well reading silently. My students greatly struggle with spelling and vocabulary skills because their reading levels are so low. I have been working on incorporating more vocabulary into our curriculum, and my students are doing well and barely even realize all they are learning. It is great to be sneaky and have fun learning all at the same time! Overall, I have really enjoyed this year. Thank you to all of you for sharing your thoughts!		

can be taught, and ultimately improved thought will result in professional actions.

CHAPTER SUMMARY

In this chapter, an overview of the research is presented on reflective practice, the combination of critical-thinking standards with reflection, and opportunities to evaluate reflection. The phases of reflective thinking are described, coupled with critical-thinking standards, to train professionals to be reflective practitioners. The impact that reflection can have on future actions is detailed. Reflection can change ways of thinking through guided practice by using critical-thinking standards.

Discussion opportunities are provided for individuals to collaborate and reflect at each phase. Implications to illustrate the possible effects on professional decisions, actions, and goals are directly tied to critical thinking and reflective practice. The positive impact of understanding each phase of reflection will assist in the ability to use reflection in a more effective manner.

The critical-thinking universal standards combined with reflection by using questions and probes are an excellent way to enhance professional reflections. Through extensive practice with critical-thinking skills applied to the reflective phases and by either questioning personal actions or by having a peer or colleague work in cognitive coaching, reflections can change an individual's professional life and ultimately the success of others.

CHAPTER STUDY QUESTIONS

After reading this chapter, use these questions to discuss with your colleagues:

1. How does experience and background knowledge influence reflection?
2. How can a professional examine personal reflections and use the criteria of phases to make knowledgable choices that will influence current and future actions?
3. After examining each phase of reflection, name or list some key attributes of each phase.
4. Define critical thinking, and list ways critical thinking enhances reflection.
5. List the Universal Standards of Critical Thinking and provide examples of each related to a personal experience.

PROBLEM SETS/ACTIVITIES

Group participants into teams of two, and follow the directions for the different problem sets/activities. Paper and pencil may be needed for this activity.

1. Read the following reflections posted on a teacher blog and categorize each phase of reflection. (Refer back to this chapter to the descriptions of each phase, if needed.)
   - What are some key words or phrases in the blog that will assist you in determining which reflection phase is represented in the scenario?
   - Use some critical-thinking questions or prompts and respond to this reflective blog in a way that will improve the reflection.

Reflection Blog # 1

One of my concerns today was how do I know when adding my own side notes will be beneficial, and at what point in the lesson am I overloading my students? After several minutes in the lecture, I feel that I am forcing comments and teaching points, and the students really are not gaining anything from it anyway. I think about stopping, and then I think about the state assessments, and I keep trudging forward.

Reflection Blog # 2

This week has been a very stressful week. My fifth-grade class is a complete terror! One female student in particular, Katy, refuses to listen, has behavior management problems, and is rude. My class is almost impossible to teach if she is having one of her *days*. I am at a loss about which technique to try for dealing with her behaviors; Katy can be physically aggressive.

Reflection Blog # 3

I have different reading groups in my classroom, and one group is having extreme problems with fluency. I have tried a few different techniques, but I need a structured program that will work on both rate and expression. I plan to spend the next few days on reading articles, talking to my friends, and trying to find a new program.

BIBLIOGRAPHY

Argyris, C. (1992). *Reasoning, learning, and action: Individual and organizational.* San Francisco: Jossey-Bass.

Brookfield, S. (1995). *Becoming a critically reflective teacher.* San Francisco: Jossey-Bass.

Bruner, J. S. (1966). *Toward a theory of instruction.* New York: W. W. Norton and Company, Inc.

Davey, B. (1983). Think aloud: Modeling the cognitive processes of reading comprehension. *Journal of Reading, 27,* 44–47.

Dewey, J. (1916). *Democracy and education.* New York: Macmillan.

Dewey, J. (1933). *How we think.* Chicago: Henry Regnery.

Dewey, J. (1964). The relation of theory to practice in education. In R. Archambault (Ed.), *John Dewey on education: Selected writings* (pp. 313–338). Chicago: University of Chicago Press. (Original work published in 1904.)

Elder, L., & Paul, R. (2008). *The miniature guide to critical thinking, concepts, and tools*. Dillon Beach, CA: The Foundation of Critical Thinking Press.

Gagné, R. M. (1968). Learning hierarchies. In M. D. Merrill (Ed.), *Instructional design: Readings* (pp. 118–131). Englewood Cliffs, NJ: Prentice-Hall.

Ghaye, T., & Ghaye, K. (1998). *Teaching and learning through critical reflective practice*. London: David Fulton.

Piaget, J. (1967). *Six psychological studies*. New York: Random House.

Richardson, V. (1990). The evolution of reflective teaching and teacher education. In R. Clift, W. R. Houston, & M. Pugach (Eds.), *Encouraging reflective practice in education* (pp. 3–19). New York: Teachers College Press.

Ross, D. D. (1990). Programmatic structures for the preparation of reflective teachers. In R. Clift, W. R. Houston, & M. Pugach (Eds.), *Encouraging reflective practice: An examination of issues and exemplars* (pp. 98–118). New York: Teachers College Press.

Schön, D. (1983). *The reflective practitioner*. New York: Basic Books.

Schön, D. (1987). *Educating the reflective practitioner*. San Francisco: Jossey-Bass.

Tennyson, R. D. (1990). Cognitive learning theory linked to learning theory. *Journal of Structured Learning, 10*, 249–258.

Tennyson, R. D. (1992). An educational learning theory linked to instructional design. *Educational Technology, 32* (1), 36–41.

Valli, L. (1992). *Reflective teacher education: Cases and critiques*. New York: State University of New York Press.

van Manen, M. (1977). Linking ways of knowing with ways of being practical. *Curriculum Inquiry, 6,* 205–228.

Wertsch, J. V. (1979). From social interaction to higher psychological processes: A clarification and application of Vygotsky's theory. *Human Development, 22,* 1–22.

Zeichner, K. M., & Liston, D. P. (1996). *Reflective teaching: An introduction*. Mahwah, NJ: Lawrence Erlbaum Associates, Inc.

Chapter Seven

Reflection and Leadership

"Reflective practice is essential if we are serious in our desire to deal with teaching and teaching practice not merely as a technical activity, but as a professional one" (Reagan, 1993, p. 195).

OVERVIEW

Leadership of the school sets the tone for the entire school community. Reflective practice by the leader is imperative to a successful and effective learning environment. Three areas of reflective practice by school leaders are the focus of this chapter. The process of reflective decision making is explored. School climate, new teacher mentoring, and reflective evaluation using electronic portfolios and written journals are examined, analyzed, and related to the development of professional growth plans. School leadership is one of the most important influences on student achievement. Reflective leaders are seen as effective leaders, positively impacting teacher morale and student achievement.

REFLECTION AND THE LEADER

Effective organizational leaders improve practice, working environments, and professional development by expanding the power of reflection. These leaders typically use reflective practice to build a community of effective teachers. By expanding thoughts and understandings of reflection, professional leaders are able to infuse the power of reflective practice into the school culture. Reflective practice by the leader is imperative to a successful and effective learning environment (Lashway, 1996). Effective leaders:

- examine by framing and reframing an event, problem, or situation of the workplace to resolve dilemmas of professional practice with effective decision making.
- develop an awareness of the dispositional, contextual, and experiential aspects of critical reflection.
- develop a climate that promotes, supports, and envelops reflective practice as a tool for developing a shared vision.
- question personal assumptions and values.
- assume responsibility for personal and professional development.

REFLECTIVE DECISION MAKING

School leaders facilitate the attainment of shared decision making by supporting reflective practice. The administrative leader builds upon the inclusive school climate and develops a shared decision making model that distributes leadership responsibilities to all involved. Reflective decision making involves giving all stakeholders a voice. School leaders must build on trusting relationships in order for their decisions to be supported. Patton (2008) indicated that "when good decisions are made, they take into account how actions will affect those who are involved" (p. 4).

Hart (1990) considered reflective decision making as a vigorous collaborative process in which professionals use a variety of sources of knowledge to shape actions toward accomplishing a goal. This process is typical in educational settings, and it is increasingly noticeable in other professions, such as medicine, business, and social work.

Reflective decision making is a professional activity that is characteristic of highly confident, skilled, creative, and competent instructional leaders. Reflective thinking requires professionals to think carefully when applying knowledge and experience to the many everyday decisions that occur. Kruse (1997) found that reflection leads to a greater sense of self-efficacy, which has a lasting and positive effect on the quality of decisions.

Reflective decision making is a key organizer for leaders to participate in reflective dialogue. Reflective dialogue involves examining and questioning practices and school policies in the context of change. Personal experiences, professional literature, outcome data from multiple sources, and survey input from various members of the professional community are analyzed during the deliberations of decision making.

A basic challenge of reflective decision making is to regard and identify the essential elements for any changes to policy or vision while respecting the diverse philosophies and viewpoints of the respective community. The ultimate goal of reflective decision making is improving professional practice by encouraging all stakeholders to carefully analyze their actions and consistently strive to accomplish meaningful outcomes.

Effective decision making requires reflection before, during, and after the decision has been made. After analyzing and synthesizing all the perspectives impacting the decision, an individual implements the action. Deliberate reflection on the impact of the decision should be a conscious habit. Continuous reflective decision making encourages the school community to support student learning.

Pause to Think . . .

Consider a situation where you made a life-changing decision. Did you seek the input of others impacted by your decision? What type of decision-making process did you use? What were the outcomes of the decision?

CLIMATE AND REFLECTIVE PRACTICE

School climate and effective school environments are highly interrelated. Positive school climates promote teacher professional development and growth. School leaders shape a reflective school environment that promotes collaborative practice by creating a climate conducive to learning and growth. The school leader promotes a culture of caring, trust, and respect among staff and students by continually modeling reflective practice.

All members of the school community must feel connected and able to work toward common goals guided by the social, academic, and community culture of the school. The social culture of the school develops as professionals are able to work and socialize together. A sense of family develops over time. These trusting relationships enable teachers to accept opinions and thoughts that may be different from their own. Working together and learning to appreciate strengths and celebrate differences are paramount to a healthy school climate.

The environment must be supportive in nature for individuals to become reflective problem-solvers. Teachers learn how to become independent thinkers and problem-solvers by engaging in active professional learning communities. All individuals need thinking and knowledge affirmed as well as challenged and stimulated.

Effective leaders build a collaborative environment by engaging all stakeholders. They are able to cultivate a sense of community with a shared vision. "Leaders must shape and nourish cultures where teachers can make a difference and every child can learn and where there is passion and commitment to designing and promoting the absolutely best that is possible" (Peterson & Deal, 2002, p. 8). Effective leaders must assess and evaluate the professional practices of teachers to encourage an environment of collegial support that provides the impetus for collaboration, dialogue, and critical thinking.

Pause to Think . . .

Climate is essential for professional growth. Think of a professional climate in which you have worked. What are some of the attributes of the climate? Would you consider the climate to be effective for professional growth? Why or why not?

REFLECTIVE EVALUATION

Leadership of the school sets the tone for the entire school community. School leaders who support reflective practice create a tone of introspection and open-minded inquiry. School leaders who support environments of mutual trust typically have an attitude of open-mindedness, responsibility, and dedication. These attributes are associated with reflective mentoring practices.

Dewey (1933) referred to open-mindedness as an interest in listening to all sides of an issue and a willingness to question the most basic assumptions that underlie a belief or practice. Responsible and dedicated educational leaders are receptive to the professional needs of their school community, enabling teachers to develop professional goals. Responsible and dedicated leaders begin with a common vision to incorporate knowledge of the importance of building trusting relationships in the mentoring process.

To strengthen professional practice, the school leader must focus on what was learned and how that information can be used to improve teacher and student performance (DuFour & Marzano, 2009). This section is focused on professional growth opportunities in which the school leader uses reflective practice as a tool to promote growth and change. The focus areas are

- mentoring,
- electronic portfolios,
- reciprocal journals, and
- professional development.

REFLECTIVE EVALUATION: MENTORING

Many conceptions exist about mentoring. Among these conceptions are the following:

1. Mentoring as support includes the idea that mentors offer advice, listen to problems, provide emotional support, and suggest alternative instructional tools.
2. Mentoring as apprenticeship involves following the advice and modeling of the more experienced person.
3. Mentoring as on-the-job training involves the experienced mentor and the novice teacher exploring ideas together and valuing their relationship (Adapted from Koballa, Bradbury, & Deaton, 2008).

Mentoring is generally thought to be an interaction between a novice teacher and an experienced teacher. Brock (1999) noted that "the success of beginning teachers is critical to student success, and the success of both is largely the responsibility of the principal" (p. 20). School leaders should play an active role in mentoring new teachers (Tillman, 2003). New teachers need support that can only be provided by the school leader. This support includes:

- orientation to the school and standard operating procedures,
- introduction to the school's vision and goals,
- development of ways of thinking about instructional practices,
- comprehension of beliefs and behaviors of peers, students, and administrators,
- acquisition of the role the teacher plays in the school culture, and
- use of reflective practice skills.

School leaders identify the perceptions new teachers have of mentoring and address the process from their perspective to build knowledge and trust. Professional interactions between novice teachers and school leaders are impacted by the conceptual ideas each party identifies. A new teacher will be more likely to trust the mentoring process and to develop the reflective skills necessary to improve teaching when the leader is trustworthy, open-minded, and reflective.

Mentoring is an opportunity for the leader to build relationships with novice teachers, introduce them to the school's vision and goals, and encourage the development of reflective practice skills. Reflecting on practice and discussing the reflections with the leader provides the avenue for the novice teachers to begin to effect change in pedagogy. In addition, the mentoring process provides the leader information to improve teaching and learning for professional development (Tillman, 2003).

Pause to Think . . .

Think of a time when you had a mentor. What was your perception of the mentoring process? What mentoring process did you use, and was it successful?

REFLECTIVE EVALUATION: ELECTRONIC PORTFOLIOS

The reflective electronic portfolio is defined as a flexible, evidence-based process and product that combines reflection and documented evidence. A portfolio engages individuals in ongoing self-evaluation and a collaborative analysis of application of theory to practice. The portfolio focuses on purposeful, narrative outcomes for both goal-setting and assessing practice. Individuals are asked to create, collect, select, and connect the work included into the larger framework of the institution (Zubizarreta, 2004).

Electronic portfolios are extremely useful for bridging the gap between authentic learning and educational assessment. Not only is the electronic portfolio effective for focusing on predetermined goals to achieve but also it focuses on critical inquiry that questions practice.

The outcomes of the portfolio are two-fold. Primarily, individuals become more self-aware of personal choices, including what tasks are avoided and why, what tasks attract and why, what risks are attempted and why. Secondly, portfolios are to be shared with others. Typically, high and low moments in professional growth are shown, along with conditions that exemplify that growth. Portfolios showcase the personal traits of collaboration, critical thinking, creativity, and risk taking.

Some questions that teachers may consider when preparing an electronic portfolio for submission to the principal for evaluation and feedback are

1. Do I have my own professional teaching portfolio?
2. Are my goals and objectives explicit with clear due dates?

3. Are my artifacts of appropriate length with standards and goals addressed?
4. Have I organized the portfolio in a way that is logical and saves time and effort in submission?
5. Do I incorporate other required work, such as a paper, project, or lab reports into my portfolio? For example, does my portfolio serve double duty?

Electronic portfolios offer an avenue for school leaders to encourage reflective thought and professional growth. This venue is a powerful instructional tool that will guide practice, impact student learning, and provide opportunities for improvement. Electronic portfolios offer the opportunity for teachers to recap lessons, reflect on the outcomes of those lessons, explore related literature for improvement on current practice, and share thoughts with school leaders for comments and suggestions.

Portfolios encourage reflective practice and critical thinking as teachers clarify goals, examine strengths and weaknesses, and provide documentation for growth and performance. School leaders provide reflective feedback through the portfolio as teachers examine practice and reflect on student learning. Effective school leaders devote time to guiding teachers in building their own capacity.

Portfolios encourage teachers to observe, analyze, and judge performance on the basis of established standards and reflect on how to improve practice. School leaders review teacher portfolio reflections to determine if teacher self-assessment identifies areas for improvement of professional practice. For example, after a lesson, the teacher reviewed the instruction, analyzed the learning, and made judgments on performance. The reflection from the teacher indicated that the instruction could be improved by the addition of instructional strategies aimed at keeping students on task. However, the teacher's reflection indicated an uncertainty of what strategies to include. The school leader then takes this opportunity to suggest strategies for improving the teacher's performance and maximizing student learning.

Pause to Think . . .

What are your experiences with portfolios? What are some advantages and possible disadvantages to portfolios? Write your thoughts in a journal, and then share with a friend.

REFLECTIVE EVALUATION: RECIPROCAL JOURNALS

Reciprocal journals provide an informal avenue of communication between novice teachers and leaders. Reciprocal journals are diary-type records that allow "private written conversations with each other over an extended period of time" (Tillman, 2003, p. 229). Teachers need to develop the ability to think critically. Reflection and dialogue in the form of a written reciprocal journal provide a vehicle for the development of critical-thinking and reflective-practice skills. Journals offer the opportunity for self-expression by teachers as they reflect on student learning.

School leaders use journals for critical reflection of their expectations for teachers and can encourage teacher reflection on lessons through this written medium. The journal allows the teacher to keep a continuous record of past practice and thoughts on the effectiveness of that practice. When shared with the school leader, the journal provides a means by which the leader can assess a teacher's reflective thinking skills.

Reciprocal journals encourage teachers to personalize theory into practice as they reflect upon daily activities in the classroom. These reflections provide the school leader with the opportunity to review, analyze, and guide the development of reflective practice in the classroom. Reciprocal journals stimulate interest in pedagogical tools and contribute to the learning process (Lee, 2008) while allowing the leader to observe growth in reflective practice and teacher effectiveness.

Pause to Think . . .

What do you think of journaling? How can reciprocal journals provide you feedback for improvement?

REFLECTIVE EVALUATION: PROFESSIONAL DEVELOPMENT

Making new tasks personalized requires practice and working closely with others who are invested in the new learning. Internalizing the new task is a gradual process by which the skill transfer slowly becomes self-regulated. Initially, as new behaviors and tasks are acquired, the skills are explicit and overt, and with practice and support from others, the new skill becomes self-regulated (Wertsch, 1979).

In order for individuals to become reflective problem-solvers, the environment must be supportive in nature while the novice teacher develops professionally. It is important that professionals become independent thinkers and problem-solvers by engaging in active learning opportunities with others. "Wise leaders collaborate to incorporate best practices, solve problems, and address the issues facing their organizations" (Workforce Management, 2008, paragraph 10).

REFLECTIVE EVALUATION: PROFESSIONAL GROWTH PLANS

Effective classroom instruction leads to increased student learning. Electronic portfolios and reciprocal journals provide an avenue for critical reflection by both the classroom teacher and the school leaders. These media encourage critical thinking and learning, processes required for significant professional development. By keeping continuous written logs and reflecting on the impact of instruction on student learning, professional growth plans are developed and professional practice is continually evaluated. The school leader uses the records to help guide the teacher toward appropriate self-development activities.

Effective professional development is aimed and focused on improvement in instruction that positively impacts student learning. Professional growth plans address needs of individual teachers as identified through self-reflection and leader assessment. Growth plans describe individual goals for professional development and indicate the activities and standards for expected growth. Leaders guide growth plans through the observation of teacher reflection and assessment, make periodic reviews of growth processes, and suggest strategies as the teacher progresses through the growth activities. Such professional growth plans encourage teacher autonomy while providing leader support.

The use of portfolios and journals provide the vehicle for teacher self-reflection and leader feedback. These vehicles help the teacher and the leader identify areas for improvement through professional growth activities. Through the use of portfolios and journals, teachers are provided a foundation for reflection to further development and improve practice. Portfolios and journals encourage teachers to review long-term goals relating to performance development and identify strategies and activities that ensure successful professional growth. Continuous reflection, assessment, and professional growth are fostered through the use of portfolios and journals.

Teachers, as well as other professionals, draw from a multiplicity of sources for informing practice. Over the years, instructional leaders have used a variety of resources to evaluate the effectiveness of their staff and the academic achievements of their students. Listed are some of the typical methods of administrative evaluation:

- Administrative observations—typically time and date for observation are announced to the teacher prior to the classroom visit and are very subjective.
- Teacher checklists—a list of objectives the school or district determined are necessary for all teachers to achieve. The administrator checks the perceived accomplishments and discusses them with each teacher individually.
- Self-evaluation list—teacher is asked to complete a list of goals or competencies achieved from a premanufactured list, followed by a meeting and discussion with the administrator.
- Walk-through visits—usually a visit for the school administrator that is subjective and unannounced. Very little or no productive feedback is provided to the teacher. Additionally, the teacher has limited opportunities for reflection.

Historically, these evaluation practices require teachers to meet minimum standards that were not personalized to the professional needs of the teacher. These practices affected everyone but successfully evaluated no one. For sustained and effective improvement in professional practice, individuals must look inward at themselves, then outward at the environmental situation around them, and then back inward again.

Administrators began to explore alternatives for teacher evaluation and improvement of practice. They were interested in a strong and individualized professional development process because they recognized the strong correlation of student achievement to high-quality teachers and their practice. Effective administrators not only want teachers to step back and examine how they teach but also, more importantly, why they teach in that particular way and how their practice affects student achievement.

There are many variations among teachers and experience levels. The context in which the teacher is working is very important. Diversity in the classroom, teacher-student ratio, and learning styles of the students impact teacher effectiveness. For improvement of practice, teachers need to evaluate past actions, present situations, and resulting outcomes. One effective tool for self-evaluation is the use of professional growth plans.

The development of professional growth plans encourages individuals to apply what they know from theory and actual practice. In order to generate new ideas and use the *patterns of knowing* to improve their personal and professional practice, teachers can use professional growth plans. Four patterns used in the concise reflection of each goal are adapted from Carper's (1978) work on fundamental *patterns of knowing*:

- empirical—These patterns consist of scientific and evidence-based research. Teachers continuously read and develop awareness of current research in their fields of study.
- esthetic—Discover new ideas from pedagogical tact and direct experiences in practice. Teachers try different methods, materials, and techniques to improve instruction.
- ethical—This way of knowing involves moral issues and decisions. Teachers must be aware of any bias in personal and professional decision making, referred to as critical reflection.
- personal—Discovery of the inner self in relationships and associations with others. Teachers achieve personal awareness by dialoguing with others, developing a sense of self, and forming frames of reference for self-worth.

These *patterns of knowing* provide a framework that allows professionals to effectively move through the dispositional, contextual, and experiential elements involved in reflective growth (Carper, 1978). The plan is specifically designed for the particular needs of individual teachers and is equally valuable for novices as well as experienced teachers.

Pause to Think . . .

Consider the elements of a professional growth plan. With a partner, outline the elements of a professional growth plan. How can a professional growth plan be used as a guide for professional growth?

CHAPTER SUMMARY

Reflective leadership is vital to a successful school. Reflective decision making, reflective evaluation, and school climate are areas that impact student success. Reflective leaders identify sources of data that impact these areas and take action that creates the most effective and positive environment for the community.

Electronic portfolios and reciprocal journals are key vehicles for reflection and communication. These tools guide activities in practice and provide vital information for the development of professional growth plans.

CHAPTER STUDY QUESTIONS

After reading this chapter, answer the following:

1. Why is reflection important in the decision-making process?
2. How is the leader important in the mentoring process?
3. What impact does school climate have on reflective practice?
4. How can electronic portfolios be used to encourage reflective thought on professional practice?
5. Why are professional growth plans important? Describe how they help improve practice.

PROBLEM SETS/ACTIVITIES

Consider the situations below. Reflect on the questions.

1. You are the new principal at Franklin Middle School. Within the first weeks of the school year you realize that teacher morale is low, students are unhappy, and the community is withdrawn. Is this environment conducive to student achievement? Why or why not?
2. You are a teacher at Elm Hill Elementary. The principal has completed a series of evaluations on your performance and has asked you to complete a professional growth plan. How do you identify needs for a growth plan? Why are professional growth plans important?

BIBLIOGRAPHY

Balch, B. V., Frampton, P. M., & Hirth, M. A. (2006). *Preparing a professional portfolio: A school administrator's guide*. Boston: Pearson Education, Inc.

Begley, P. T. (2006). Self-knowledge, capacity, and sensitivity: Prerequisites to authentic leadership by school principals. *Journal of Educational Administration, 44*, 570–589.

Boud, D., Keogh, R., & Walker, D. (1985). Promoting reflection in learning: A model. In D. Boud, R. Keogh, & D. Walker (Eds.), *Reflection: Turning experience into learning* (pp. 18–40). London: Kogan Page.

Brock, B. (1999). The principal's role in mentor programs. *Mid-Western Educational Researcher, 12*(4), 18–21.

Carper, B. A. (1978). Fundamental patterns of knowing in nursing. *Advances in Nursing Science, 1*(1), 13–23.

Cohen, J., Pickeral, T., & McCloskey, M. (2009). Assessing school climate. *Education Digest: Essential Readings Condensed for Quick Review, 74*(8), 45–48.

Coombs, C. P. (2003). Developing reflective habits of mind. *Values and Ethics in Educational Administration, 1*(4), 1–8.

Dewey, J. (1933). *How we think: A restatement of the relation of reflective thinking to the educative process.* Boston: Houghton Mifflin Company.

DuFour, R., & Marzano, R. J. (2009). By promoting teacher learning in collaborative teams, a principal is far more likely to improve student achievement than by focusing on formal teacher evaluation. *Educational Leadership, 66*(5), 63–68.

Fenwick, T. J. (2004). Teacher learning and professional growth plans: Implementation of a provincial policy. *Journal of Curriculum and Instruction, 19*(3), 259–282.

Green, R. L. (2010). *The four dimensions of principal leadership: A framework for leading 21st century schools.* Boston: Allyn & Bacon.

Hart, A. W. (1990). Effective administration through reflective practice. *Education and Urban Society, 22,* 153–169.

Kidder, R. M. (2002). Moral courage in a world of dilemmas: Ethical decisions grow from a process that promotes rational discourse against emotional tensions. *School Administrator, 59*(2). Retrieved September 22, 2009 from http://findarticles.com/p/articles/mi_m0JSD/is_59_2/ai_82492229/?tag=content.

Koballa, T. Jr., Bradbury, L., & Deaton, C. M. (2008, Summer). Realize your mentoring success. *The Science Teacher, 43–47.*

Kruse, S. D. (1997). Reflective activity in practice: Vignettes of teachers' deliberative work. *Journal of Research and Development in Education, 31,* 46–60.

Lashway, L. (1996). Ethical Leadership. *Eric Digest, 107.* (ERIC Document Reproduction Service No. ED397463).

Lee, I. (2008, Winter). Fostering preservice reflection through response journals. *Teacher Education Quarterly,* 117–139.

Patton, M. C. (2008). Principles for principals: Using the realms of meaning to practice ethical leadership—national recommendations. *National Forum of Applied Educational Research Journal, 21*(3), 1–8.

Peine, J. (2007). *The educator's professional growth plan: A process for developing staff and improving instruction,* 2nd ed. Thousand Oaks, CA: Corwin Press.

Peterson, K. D., & Deal. T. E. (2002). *The shaping of school culture fieldbook.* San Francisco: Jossey-Bass, 8.

Reagan, T. (1993). Educating the "reflective practitioner": The contribution of philosophy of education. *Journal of Research and Development in Education, 26*(4), 191–196.

Richards, W. H., Diez, M. E., Ehley, L., Guilbault, L. F., Loacker, G., Hart, J. R., et al. (2008). Learning, reflection, and electronic portfolios: Stepping toward an assessment practice. *Journal of General Education, 57*(1), 32–50.

Tillman, L. C. (2003). Mentoring, reflection, and reciprocal journaling. *Theory into Practice, 42*(3), 226–233.

Wertsch, J. V. (1979). From social interaction to higher psychological processes: A clarification and application of Vygotsky's theory. *Human Development, 22,* 1–22.

Willingham, D. T. (2008). Critical thinking: Why is it so hard to teach? *Arts Education Policy Review, 109*(4), 21–29.

Workforce Management. (2008). Five standards of excellence practiced by ethical leaders. Retrieved June 5, 2008 from http://www.workforce.com/section/09/article/23/55/60_printer.html.

Zubizarreta, J. (2004). The learning portfolio: Reflective practice for improving student learning. Bolton, MA: Anker Publishing.

Subject Index

accommodation, 78, 80, 86
assimilation, 78, 80, 86

blogs, 47–54, 56–60, 71–73; comparison to wikis, 57; definition of, 48; guidelines for novices, 52; research base, 50; setting up a site, 51; use(s) of, 48, 49–50, 58

case study technique, 40; collective class reflection, 40
cognitive coaching, 63, 66, 69, 73–75, 87, 94; professional growth, 66, 73; reflective process, 73–74
communication skills, 66, 73–74; paraphrasing, 66–68; probing, 39, 43, 68; questioning, 52, 57, 66, 69, 94, 98; reflecting, 66, 67, 91; summarizing, 66
critical incident(s), 36, 38, 41, 43–44, 81–82; analysis, 37, 40–43, 44; interpretation, 36, 38, 41; questionnaire, 40; springboard for thought, 39
critical reflection, 38, 43–44; aspects of, 98; definition of, 35–36; in growth plans, 105, 107; in journals, 104. *See* critical incidents, analysis

critical thinking, 1, 67–68, 74–75, 94, 105; activities and scenarios, 23, 32; definition of, 88; dialogue, 30, 100; in blogs, 23; standards of, 89–90, 90–93; writing, 20–21. *See* phases of reflection; stages of critical reflection

dialogue, in Professional Learning Communities (PLCs), 9, 59; language and, 63–66, 68–71. *See* blogs; journal formats; reflective, dialogue

emerging literacies, 47, 48, 59

graphic organizers, 22, 27, 30

habits of thinking, 79, 88; reflective thought, 88. *See* reflective thinking

inner speech, 64
instructional strategies, 103; analogy, 25; questioning, 52, 57, 66, 69, 94, 98; self-questioning, 65, 71–72, 81, 86

SASS. *See* Schools and Staffing Survey
scaffolding, 69, 70, 74; instructional,
    69, 70
school climate, 97–99, 107–109
Schools and Staffing Survey, 8
self-regulation, 70, 71
stages of critical reflection: contextual
    36–37, 39–44, 83, 88, 98, 107;
    dispositional 36, 39, 40–44, 83, 98,
    107; experiential 36, 39, 40–44, 98,
    107

thinking aloud, 87

visual metaphors, 22, 25–26, 30;
    collage(s), 25–28, 31

wikis, 47–48, 50, 59–60; attributes, 55;
    benefits of, 55, 57; creating the wiki,
    56; definition and characteristics
    of, 54, 58; quality issues, 55. *See*
    emerging technologies

zone of proximal development, 70

About the Authors

Ann Shelby Harris is a professor of education at Austin Peay State University. She has taught in the public schools prior to receiving her doctoral degree and master's degree from the University of Memphis. She is a reading specialist and has taught methods classes at the undergraduate and graduate levels. She has taught online courses extensively. At the national and international levels, she is a member of the International Reading Association and the National Social Science Association. She has served six years as the International Reading Association state coordinator for Tennessee. She also served six years as editor of the state newsletter for the Tennessee Reading Association.

Harris has served as chairperson on numerous committees and in various officer positions at the international, state, and local levels. She has conducted numerous presentations at professional associations at national, regional, state, and local levels. She is very active in the local public schools, having served as a facilitator for School Improvement Projects and served as a consultant for professional development on various aspects of literacy.

Her publications include coauthor of a Phi Delta Kappan fastback titled *Managing Classroom Crises* and author of a chapter titled "Historical Trends in Bibliotheraphy: Books that Help Children Cope," in G. M. Duhon and T. J. Manson (Eds.), *Preparation, Collaboration, and Emphasis on the Family in School Counseling for the New Millennium*. She also coauthored a book titled *Capturing Change: Globalizing the Curriculum through Technology.* She has written many journal articles, funded state and national grants, and has been awarded the prestigious Outstanding Educator Award by Phi Delta Kappa and Distinguished Professor Award by the Tennessee Reading Association.

Benita Bruster is an assistant professor at Austin Peay State University in the College of Education, Department of Teaching and Learning. She currently teaches courses in literacy, curriculum and instruction, and assessment and evaluation at the graduate and undergraduate levels. Bruster has over twenty years of experience in public education. She was an elementary and middle school administrator, district-level administration and grant writer, staff developer, and classroom teacher.

Bruster currently serves as the editor for the *Tennessee Reading Teacher Journal*, and she is the president of the Mid-Cumberland Reading Council. She is an active member of the National Social Science Association (NSSA), where she serves as the editor of the newsletter for the association and a reviewer for the NSSA international journal. Bruster is also the vice-president for the Tennessee Association of Teacher Educators (TATE).

She worked for a leading technology company as a reading specialist, curriculum developer, and corporate trainer in the field of literacy. Bruster wrote and developed online interactive reading curriculum for grades kindergarten through eight that is currently used nationwide.

She has published journal articles and white papers at the state, national, and international levels on literacy, curriculum, reflection, and parental connections. Bruster has presented at local, state, national, and international conferences on reflective practice, reading comprehension and vocabulary, and teacher training.

Bruster was recently awarded Professor of the Semester by the students in the College of Education. She has received numerous grant awards for literacy and reading improvement.

Barbara Peterson is an assistant professor of education at Austin Peay State University. She has taught in the public schools prior to receiving her doctoral degree and master's degree from Northern Illinois University. She is coordinator of clinical teaching and has taught classes at the undergraduate and graduate levels, as well as online courses. At the national and international levels, she is a member of American Educational Research Association, Association for Supervision and Curriculum Development, Association of Teacher Educators, National Education Association, and National Social Science Association.

Peterson has conducted numerous presentations at professional associations at national, regional, state, and local levels. She is very active in the local public schools, developing relationships between the university and local public school districts. Her research interests include reflective professional practice, school/university partnerships, and critical thinking.

Her recent publications include authored and coauthored journal articles on reflection, mentoring, and school/university partnerships. Peterson currently serves as the advisor for the Student Tennessee Education Association.

Tammy Shutt is an associate professor in Educational Leadership Studies at Austin Peay State University. She currently teaches courses in educational leadership, educational research, and statistics at the graduate levels. Shutt has seventeen years of experience in public education. She was an executive director at the district level, an elementary school administrator, and classroom teacher prior to becoming a professor. In addition, she has ten years of experience in the public sector as a salesperson and in organizational management.

Shutt currently serves as an assistant editor for the *Journal of Interdisciplinary Education*, the journal of the North American Chapter of the World Council for Curriculum and Instruction (NAC-WCCI). She is an active member of several professional organizations, including the World Council for Curriculum and Instruction (WCCI), the Association for Supervision and Curriculum Development (ASCD), and the National Social Science Association (NSSA).

She consults with local school districts in several capacities. She participates in professional growth activities for aspiring administrators as well as practicing principals. In addition, she mentors beginning administrators as they seek to become fully licensed as professional administrators.

Shutt has published several journal articles at the national and international levels on educational leadership, ethical decision making, and teacher preparation programs. She has presented at state, national, and international conferences on reflective leadership, ethical leadership practices, electronic portfolios in leadership, and effectiveness of teacher preparation programs.